THE ULTIMATE HOW TO DRAW ANIMALS BOOK

Check us out on youtube @**Ultimate Kid Press Channel**
Share your art on facebook @**ultimatekidpress**
Let us know what you think!
Leave us a review

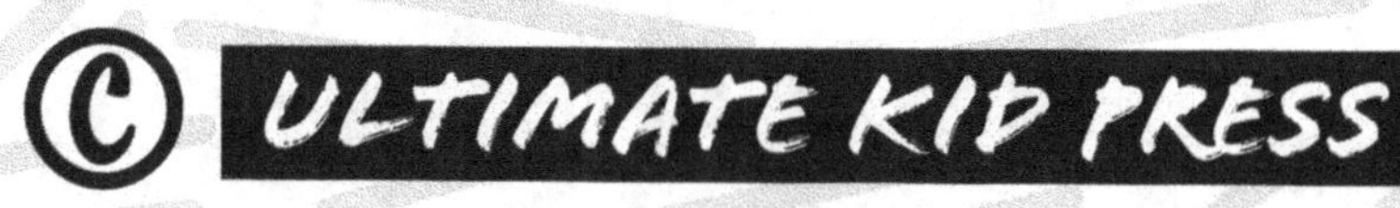

HOW TO USE THIS BOOK

1: GET A PENCIL AND AN ERASER

2: FIND A CUTE AND AWESOME ANIMAL

3: DRAW THE RED LINES FROM EACH STEP

4: AS YOU GO ERASE THE GREY LINES

5: IF YOU MAKE A MISTAKE JUST TRY AGAIN
(PRACTICE MAKES PERFECT)

TABLE OF CONTENTS

SIMPLE DESIGNS

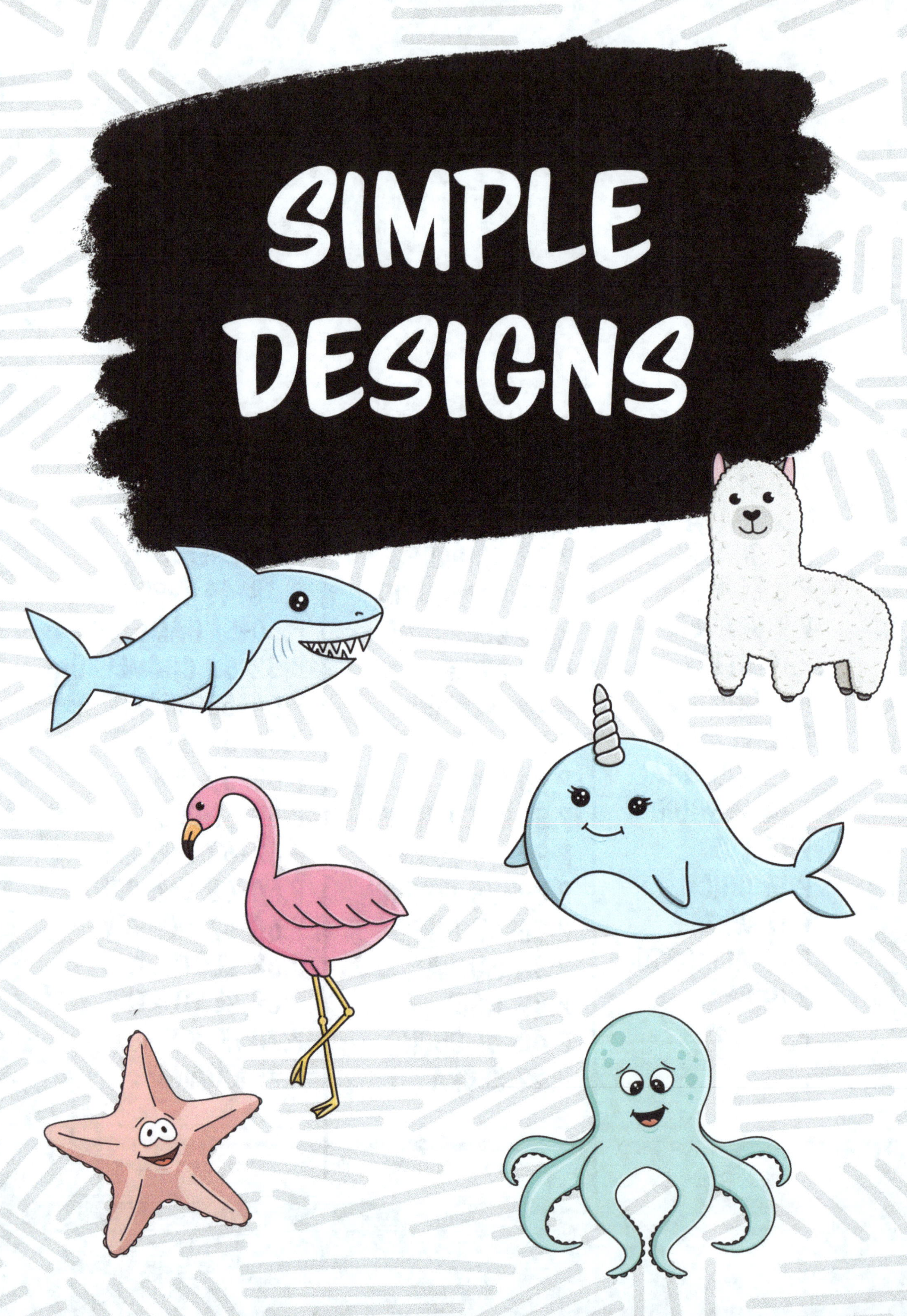

STARFISH

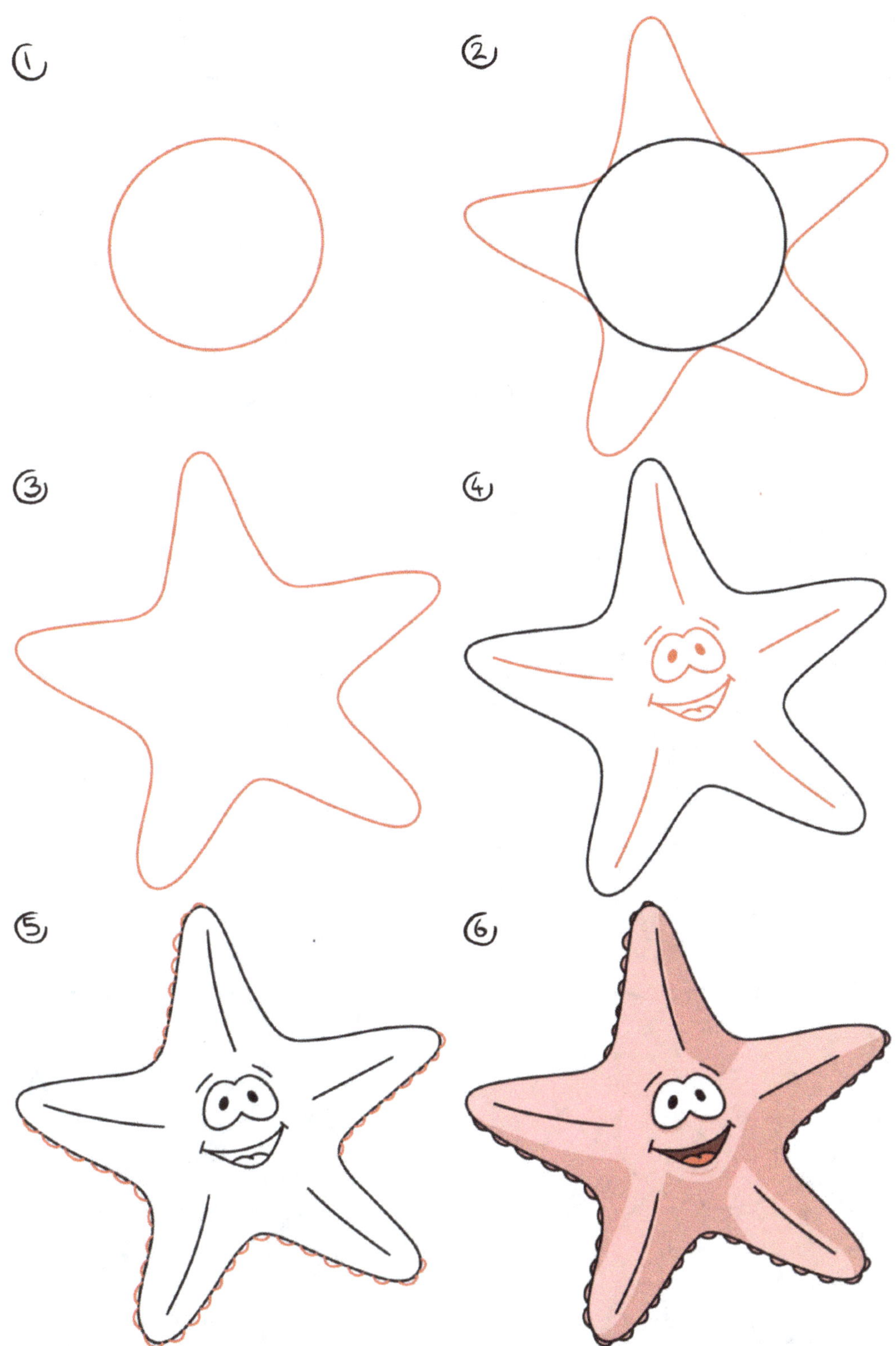

KOALA

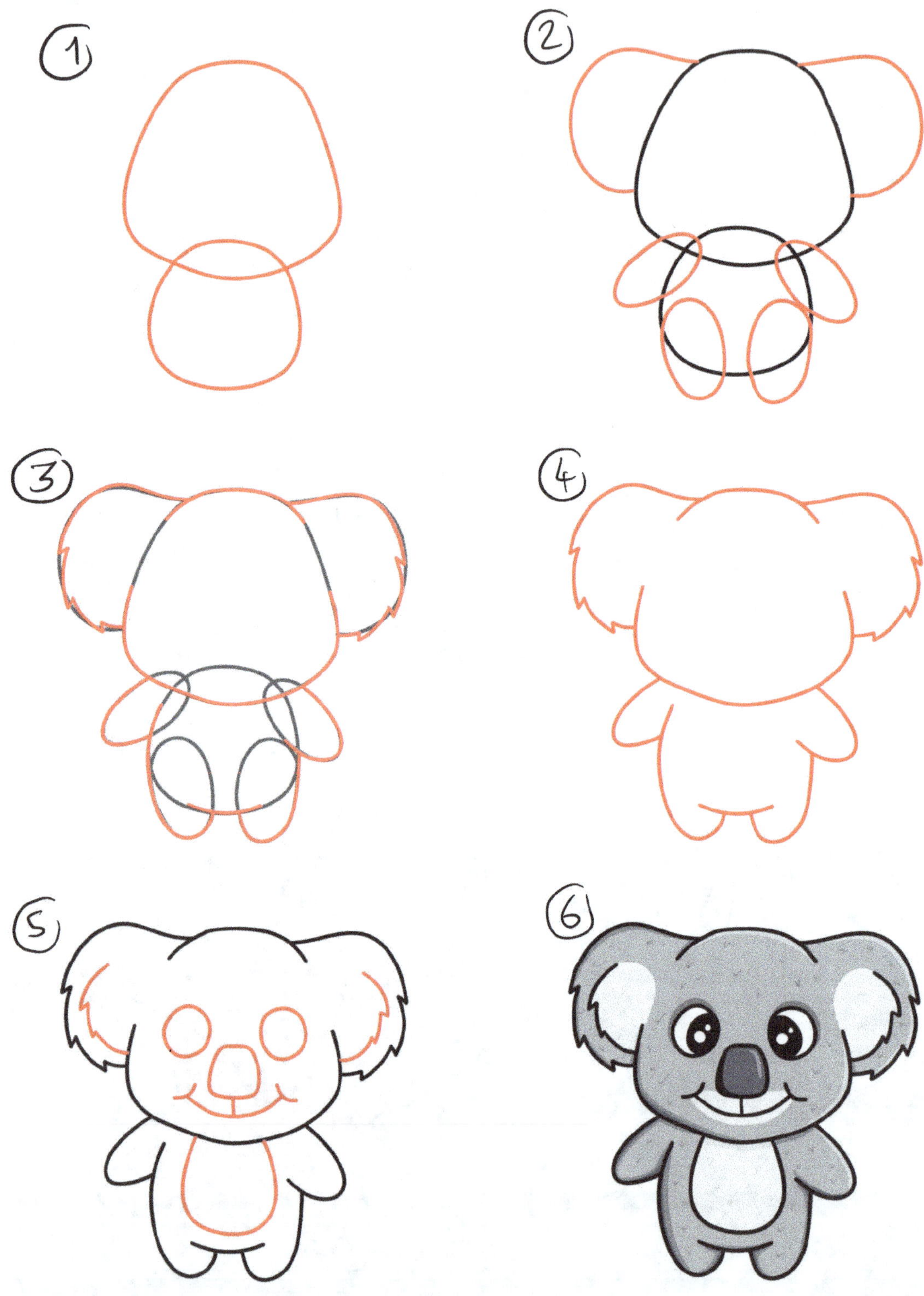

SHARK

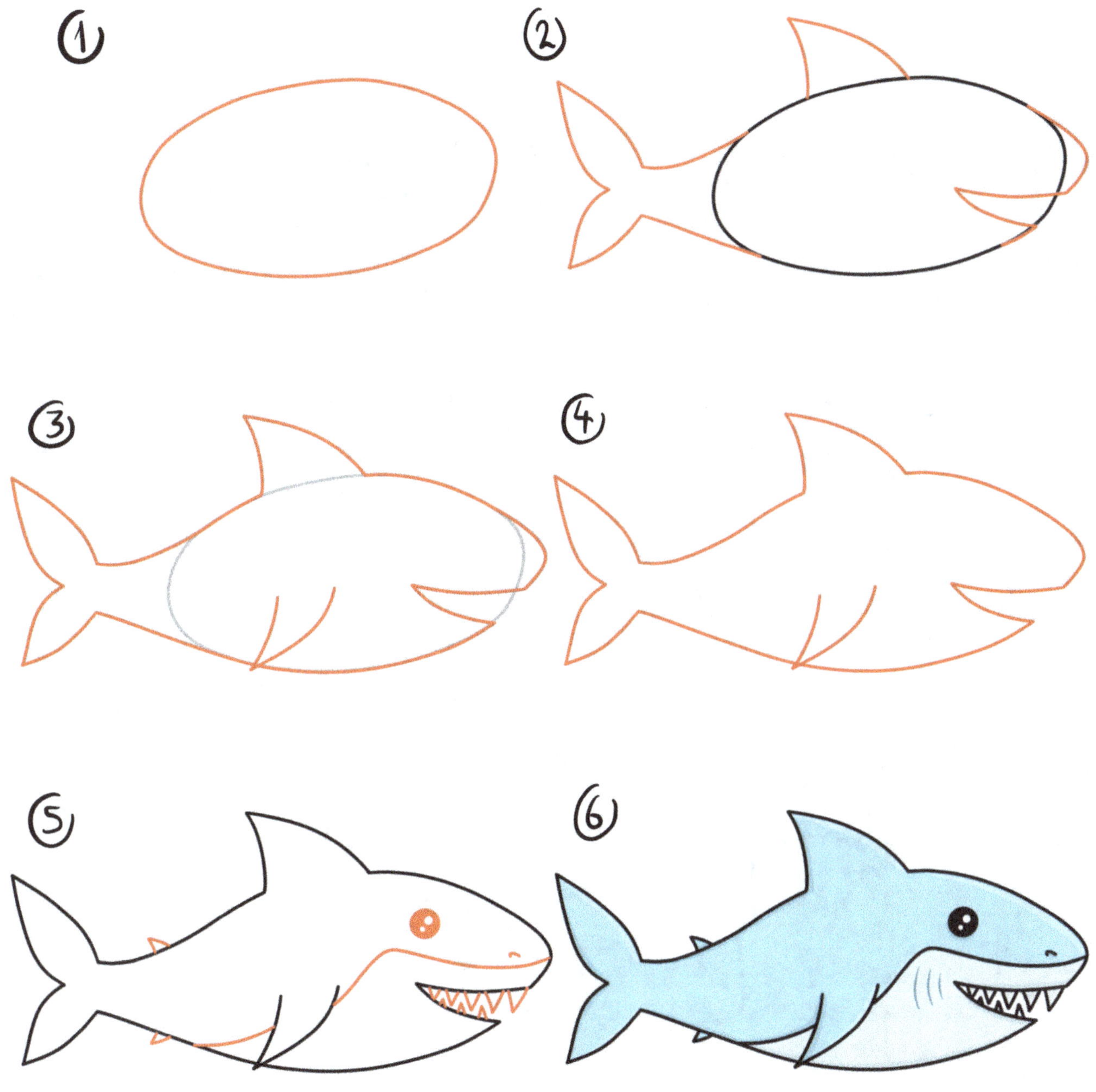

LLAMA

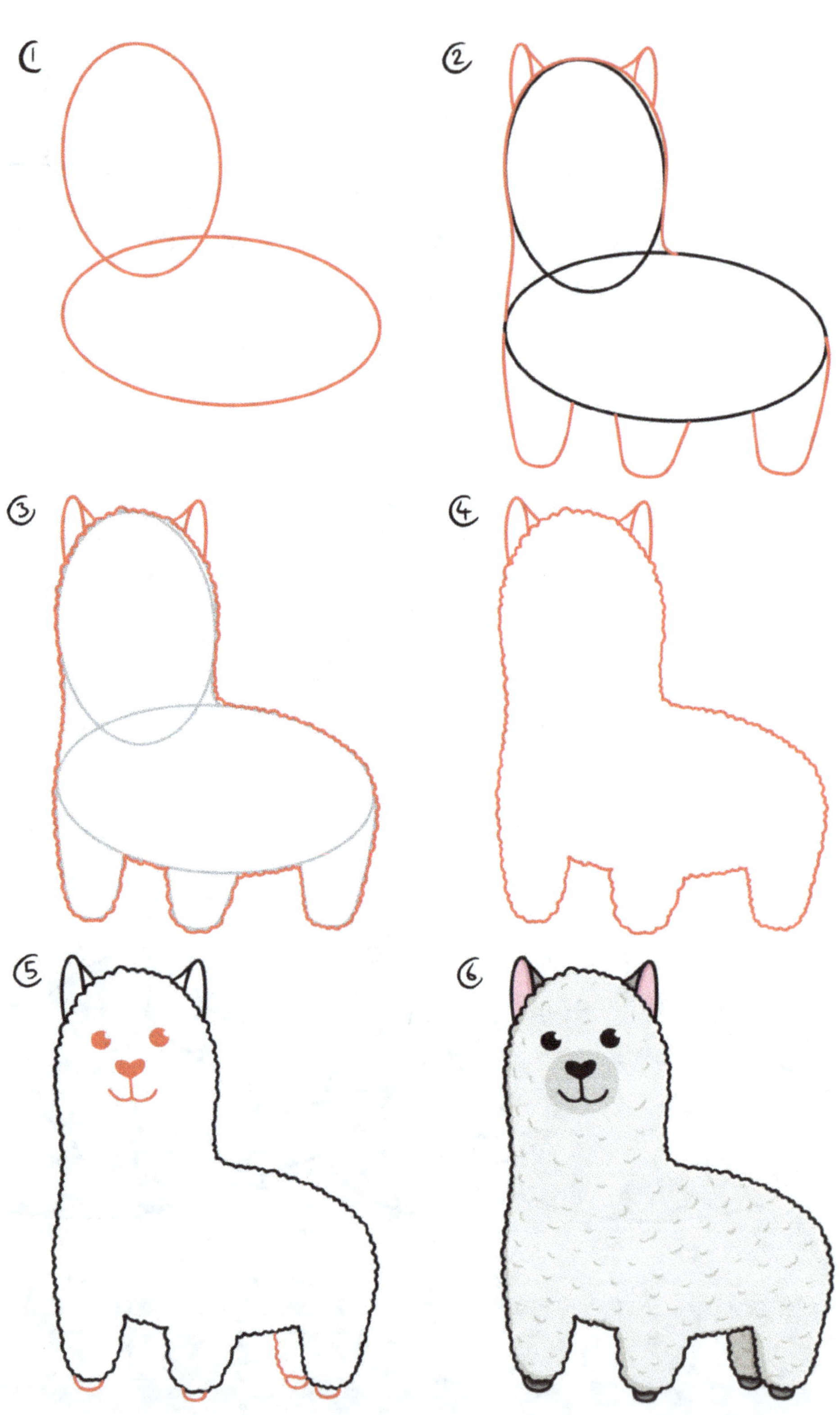

BEAVER

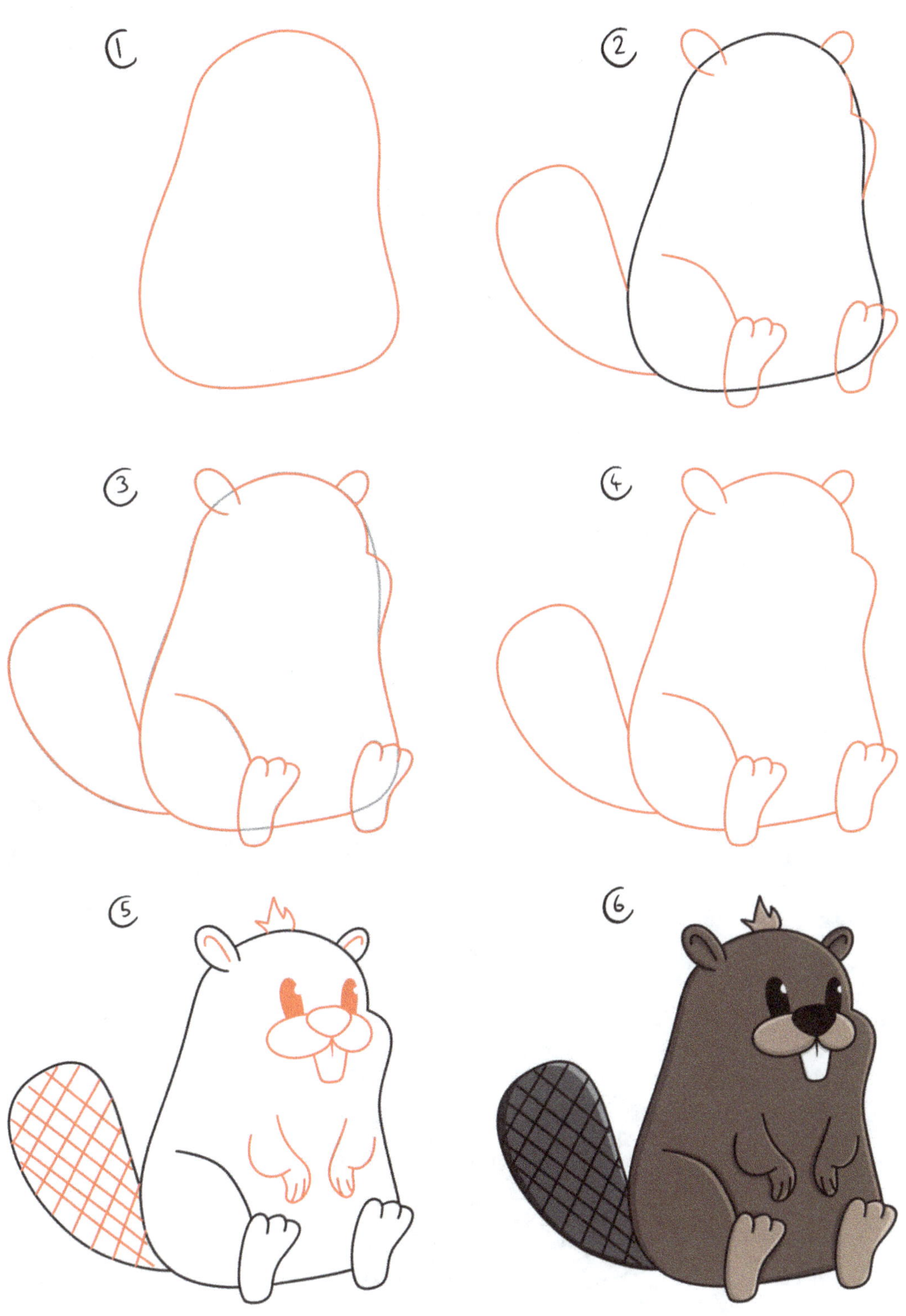

OTTER

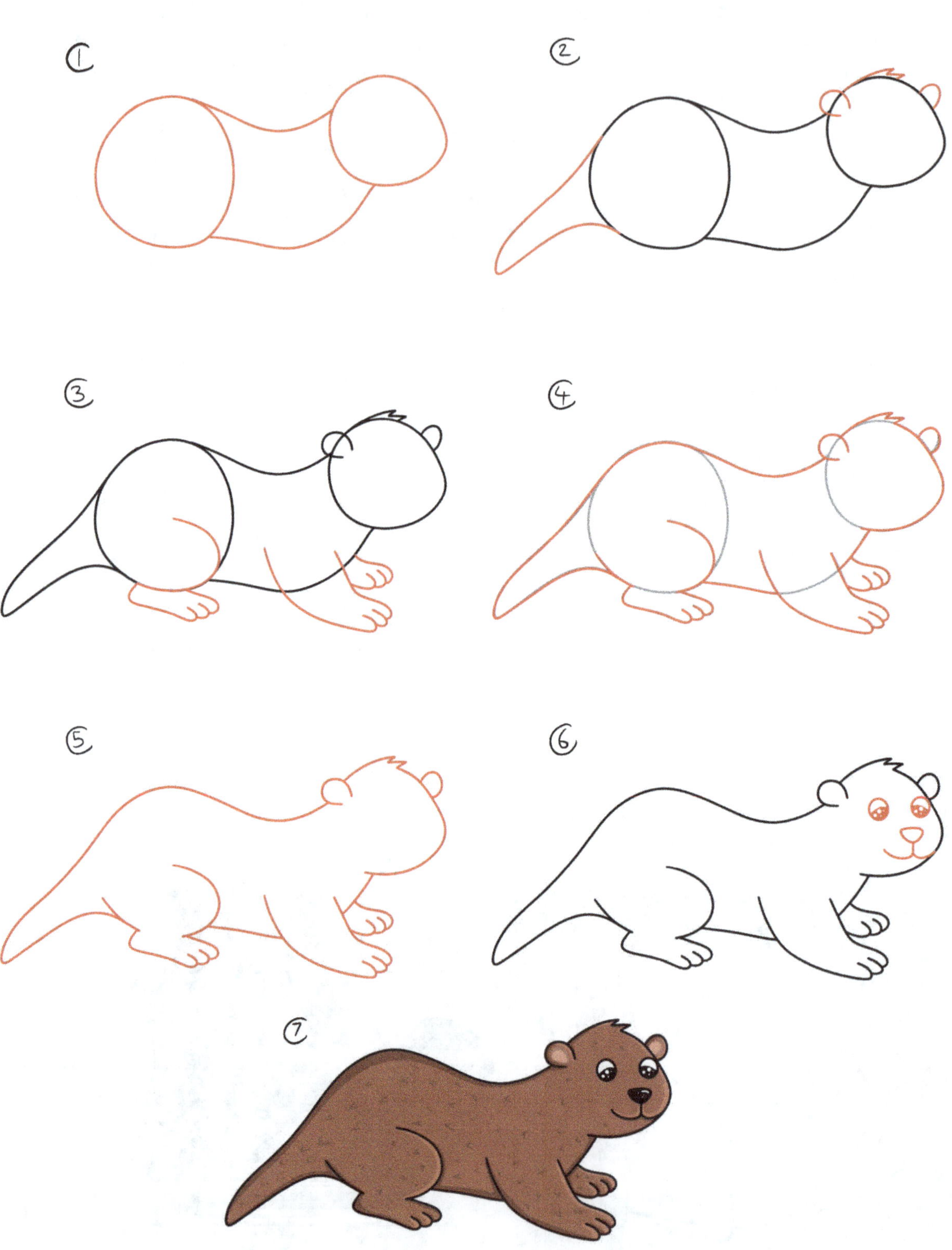

OCTOPUS

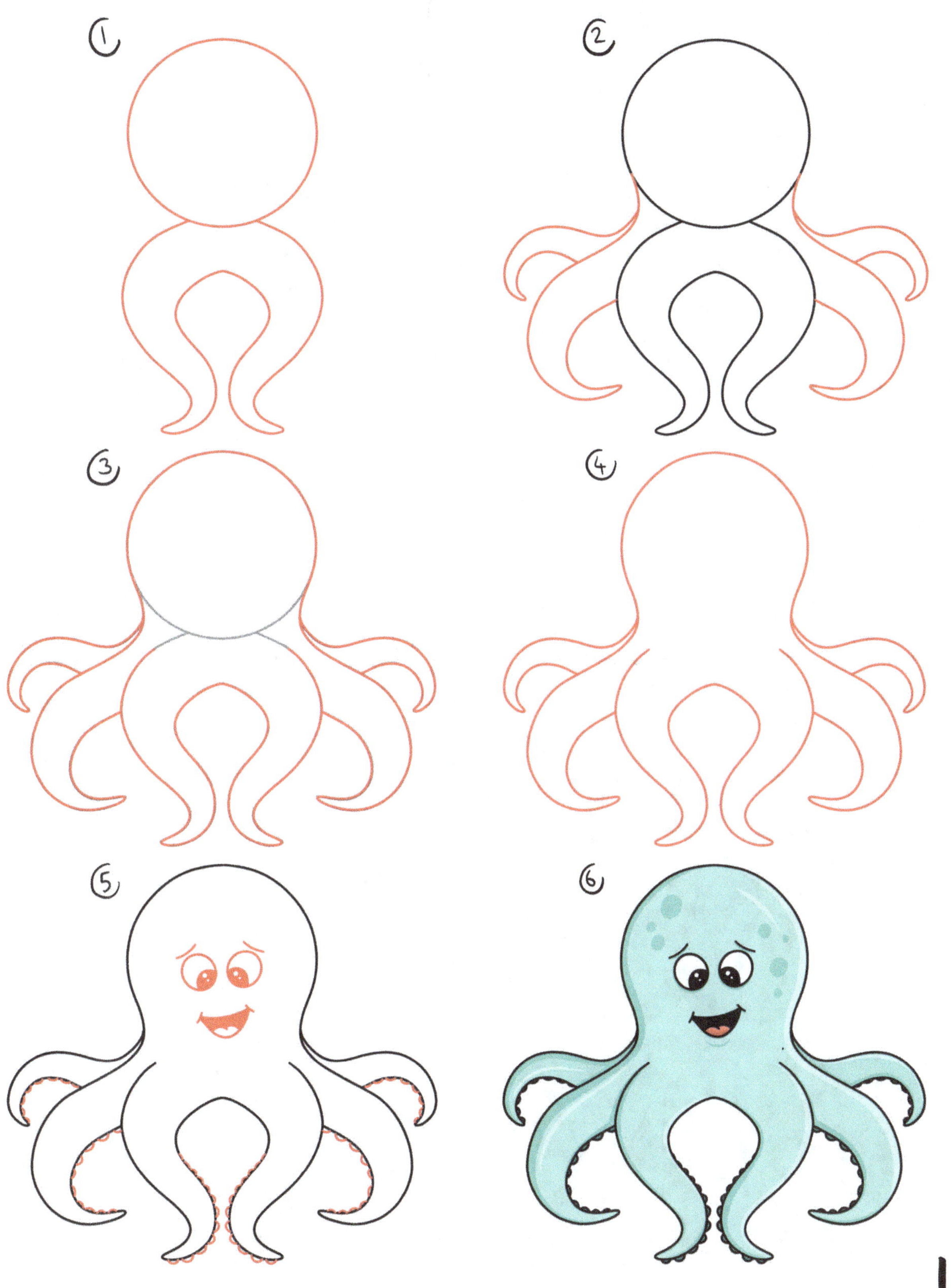

FLAMINGO

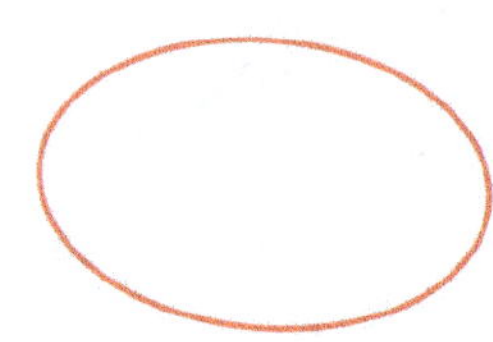

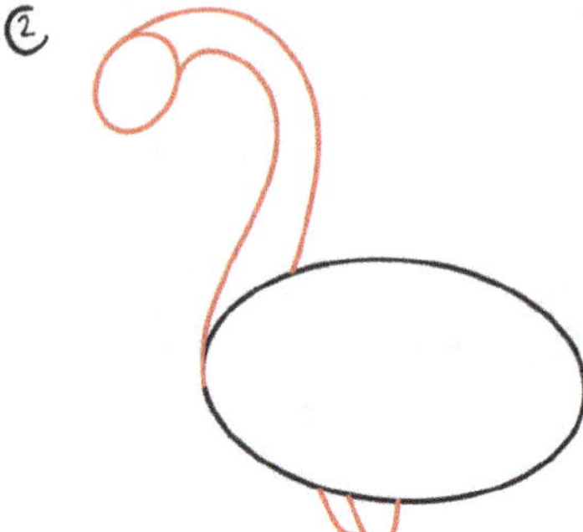

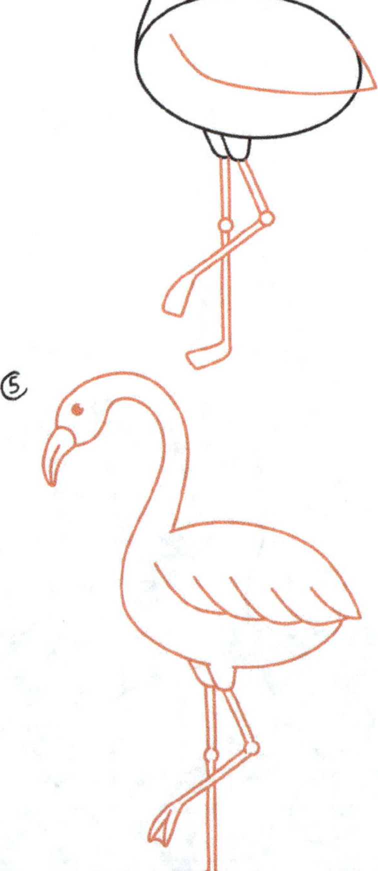

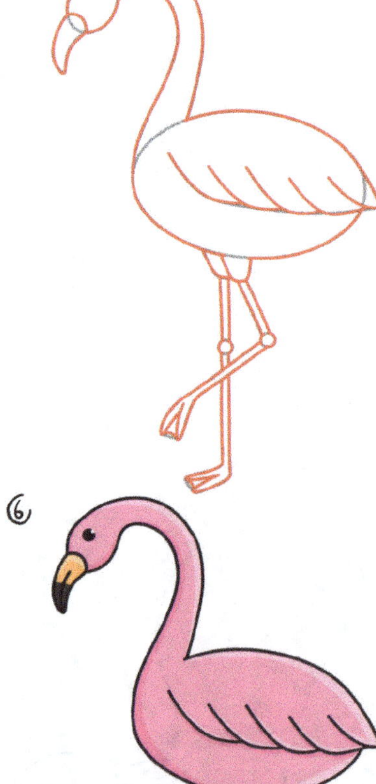

NARWHAL

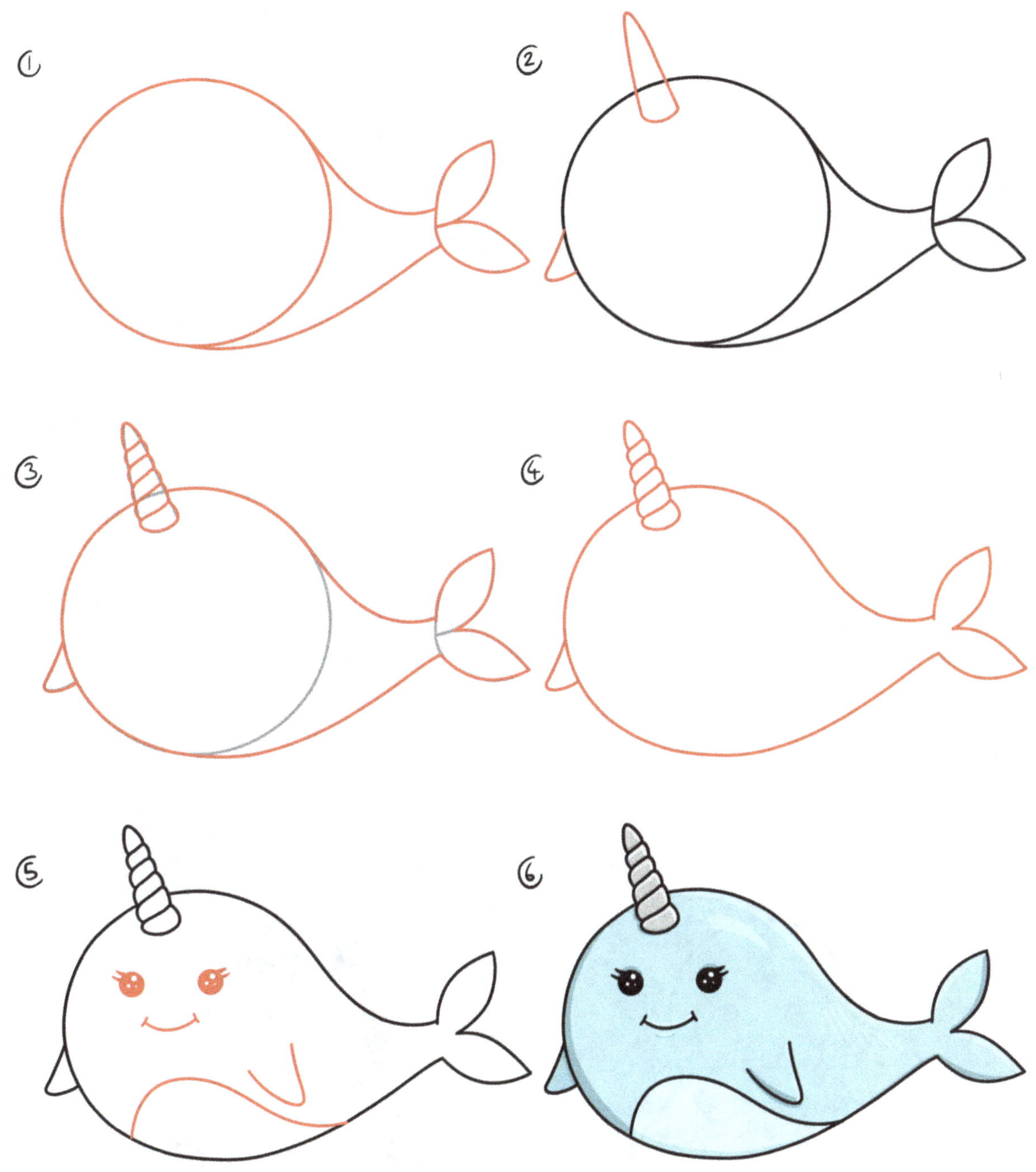

PENGUIN

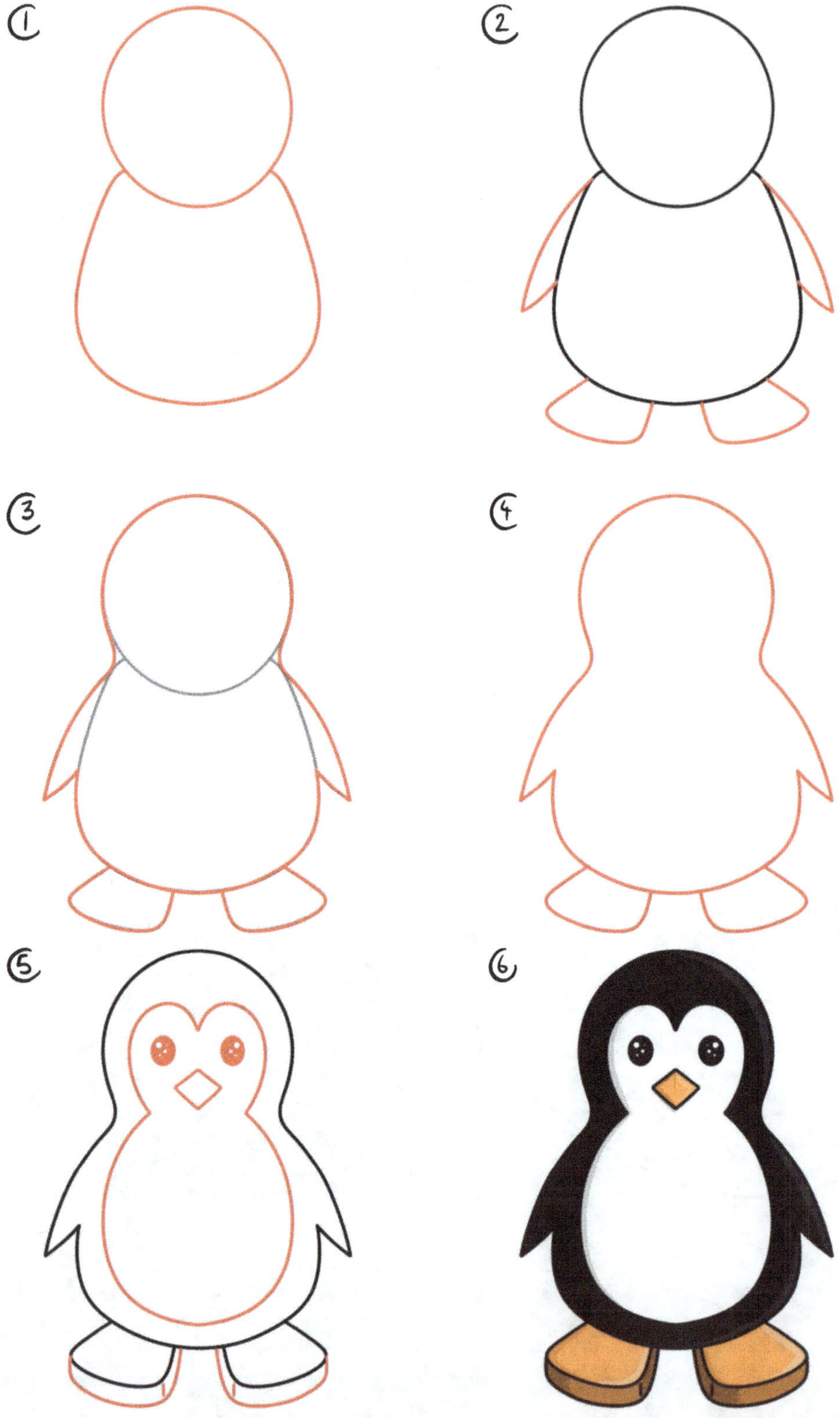

PIG

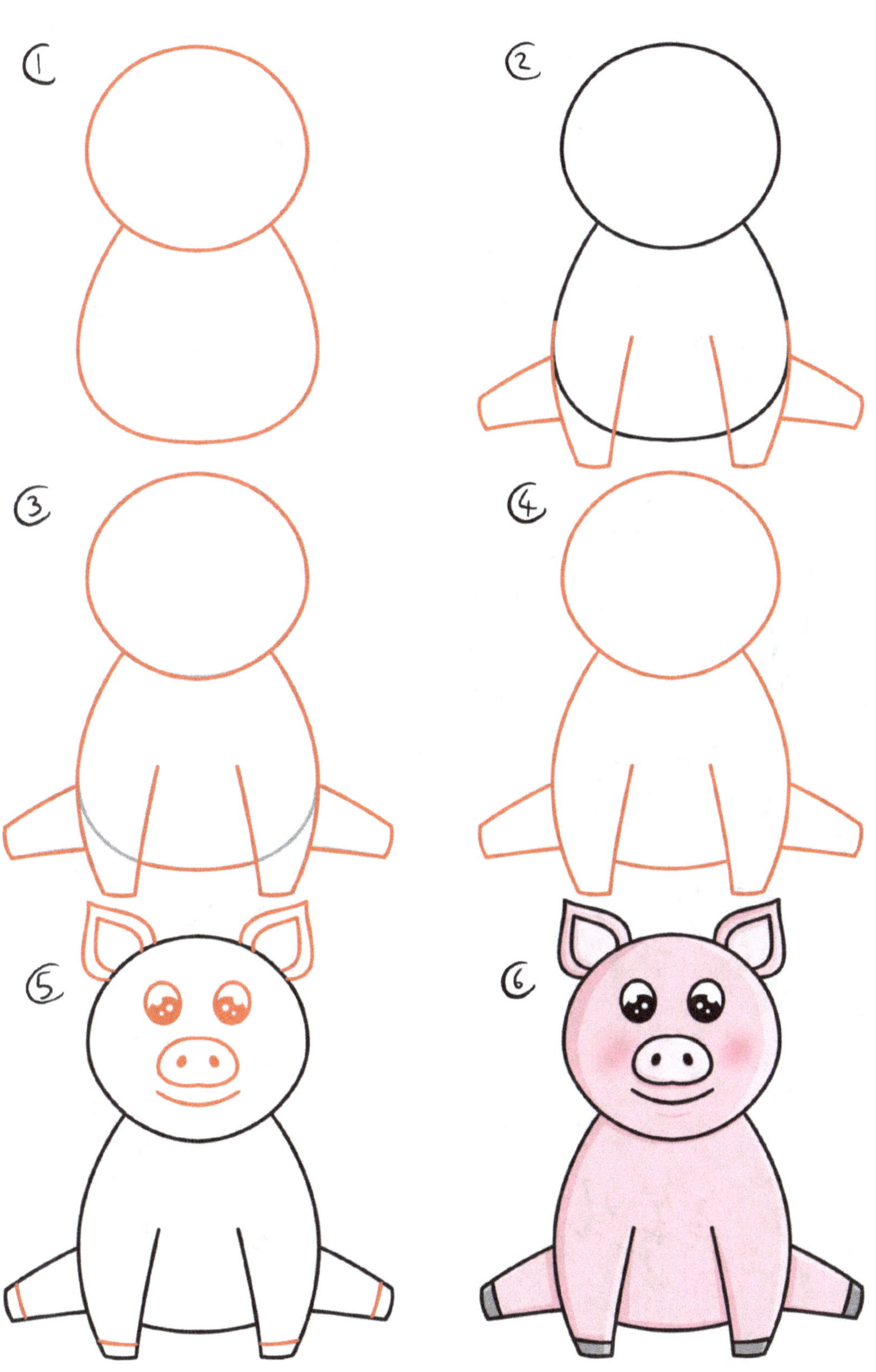

CHICK

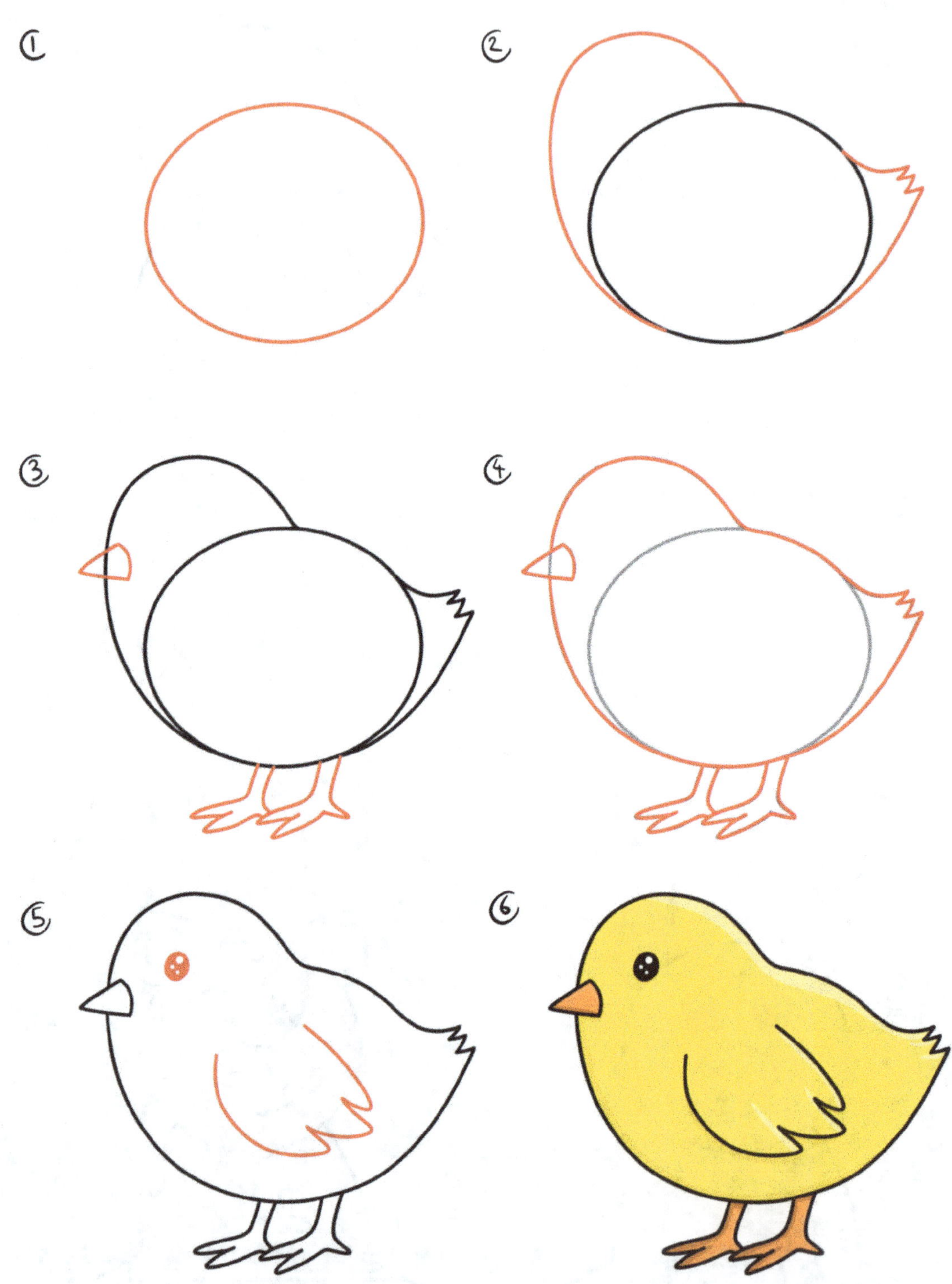

WHALE

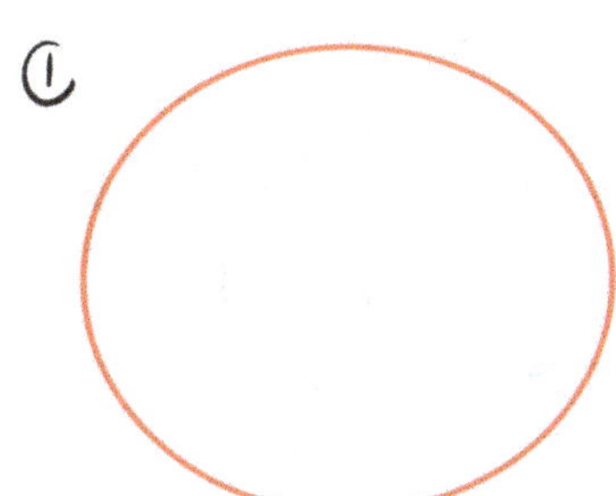

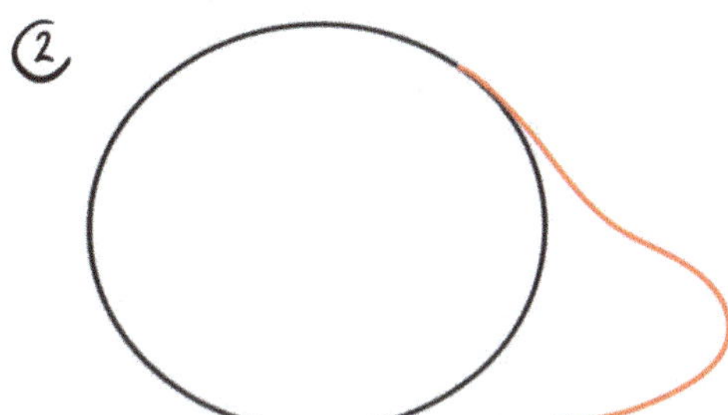

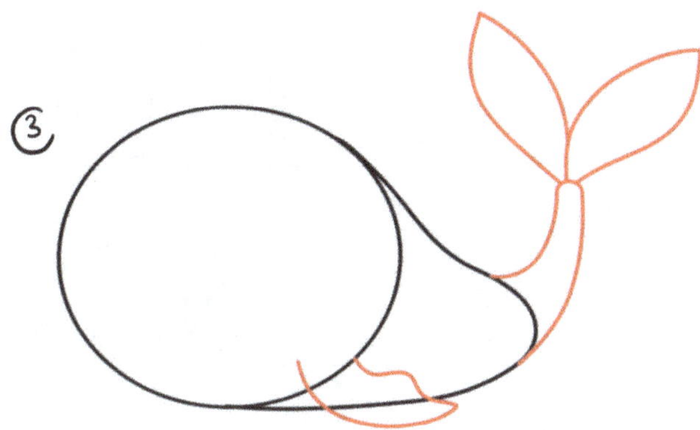

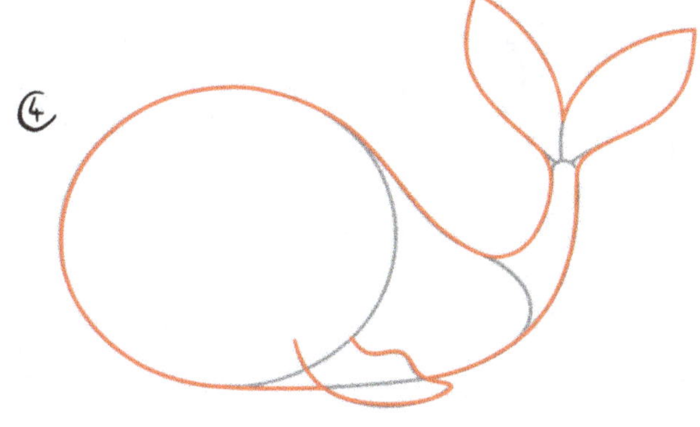

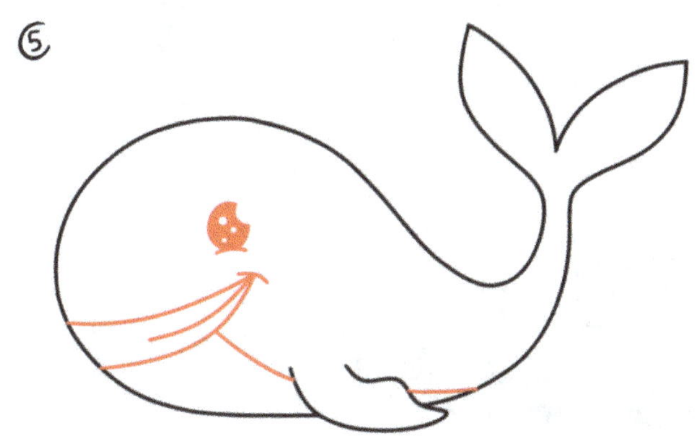

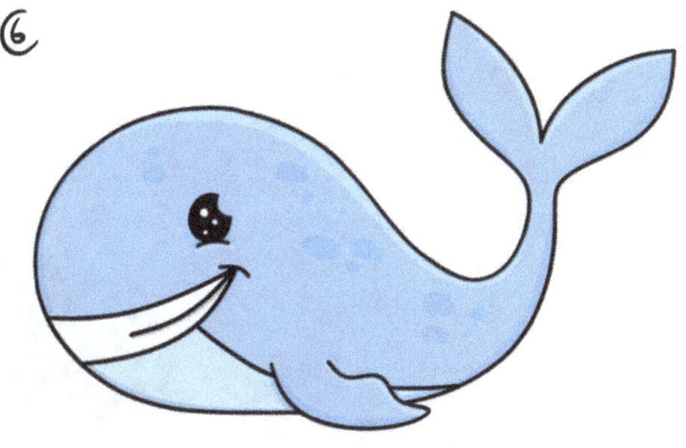

ALLIGATOR

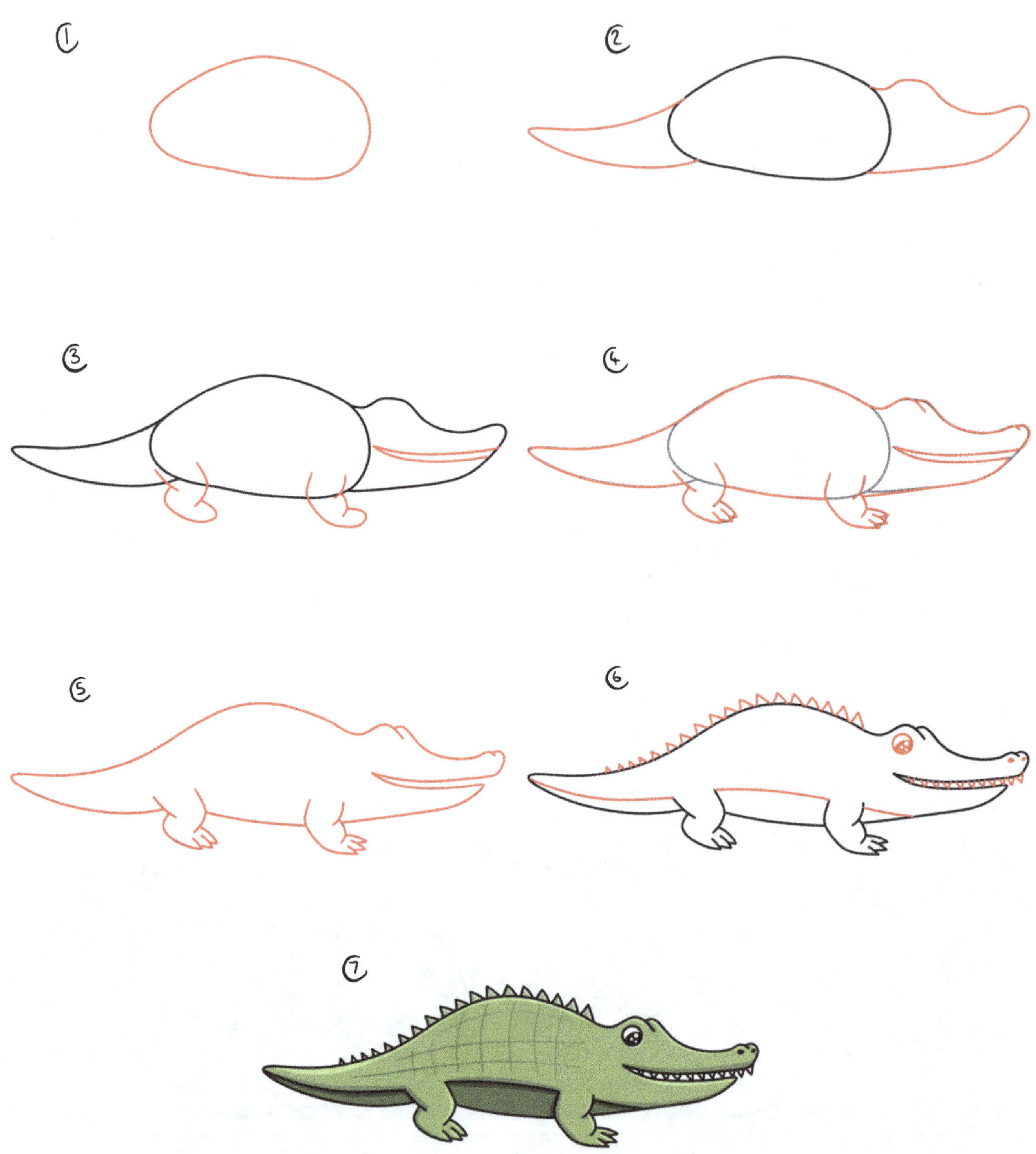

BEAR

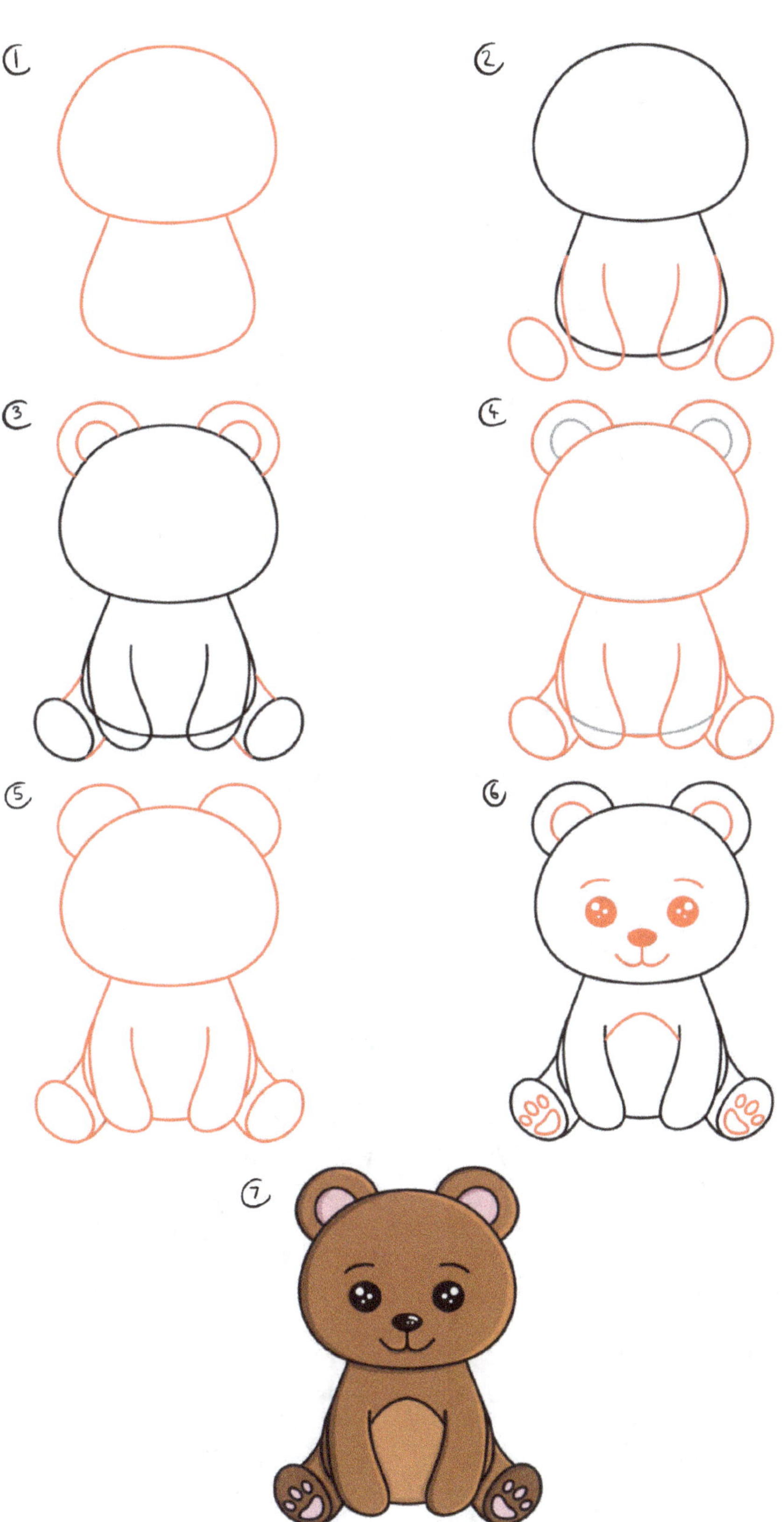

CAT

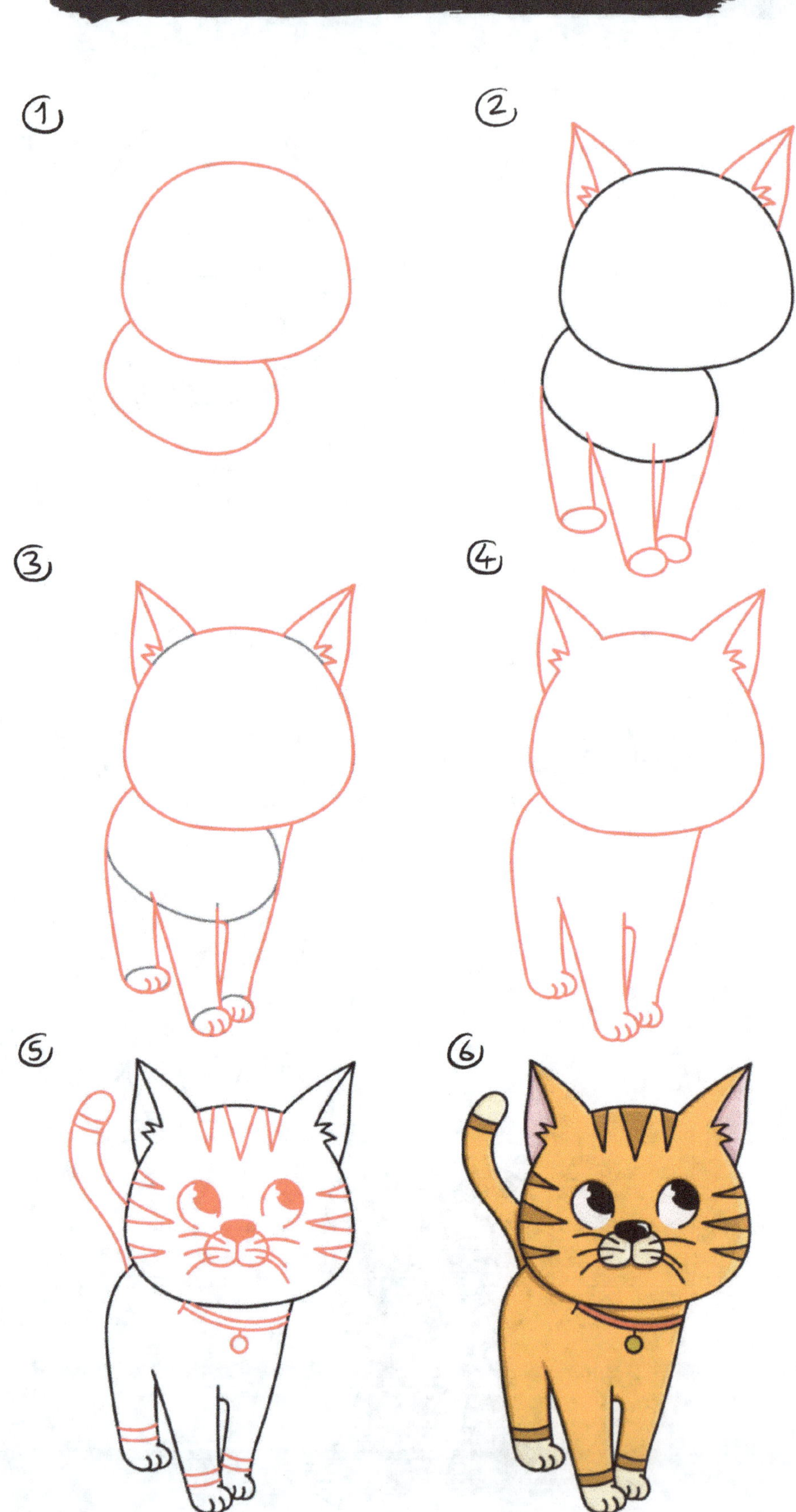

DETAILED DESIGNS

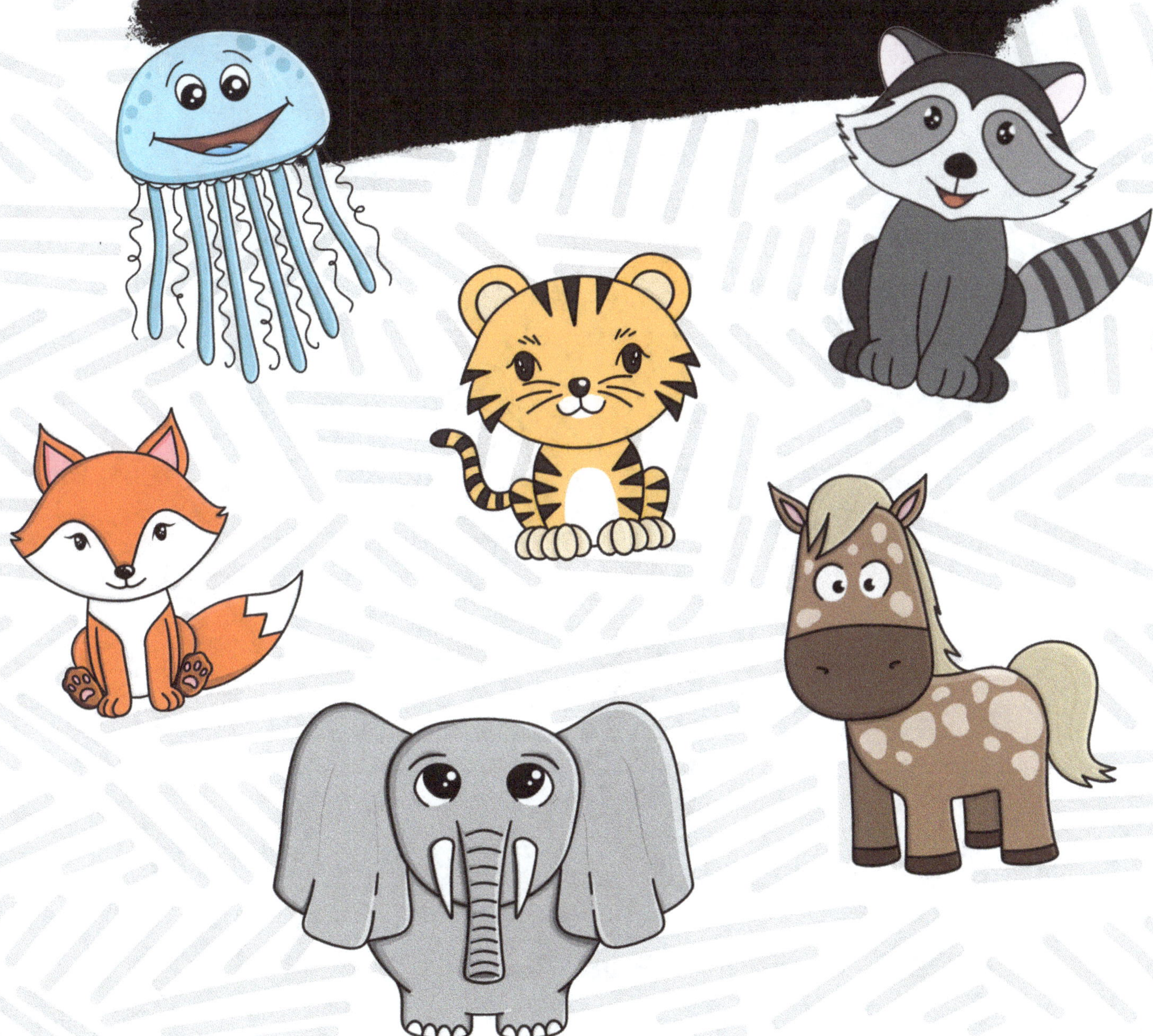

HORSE

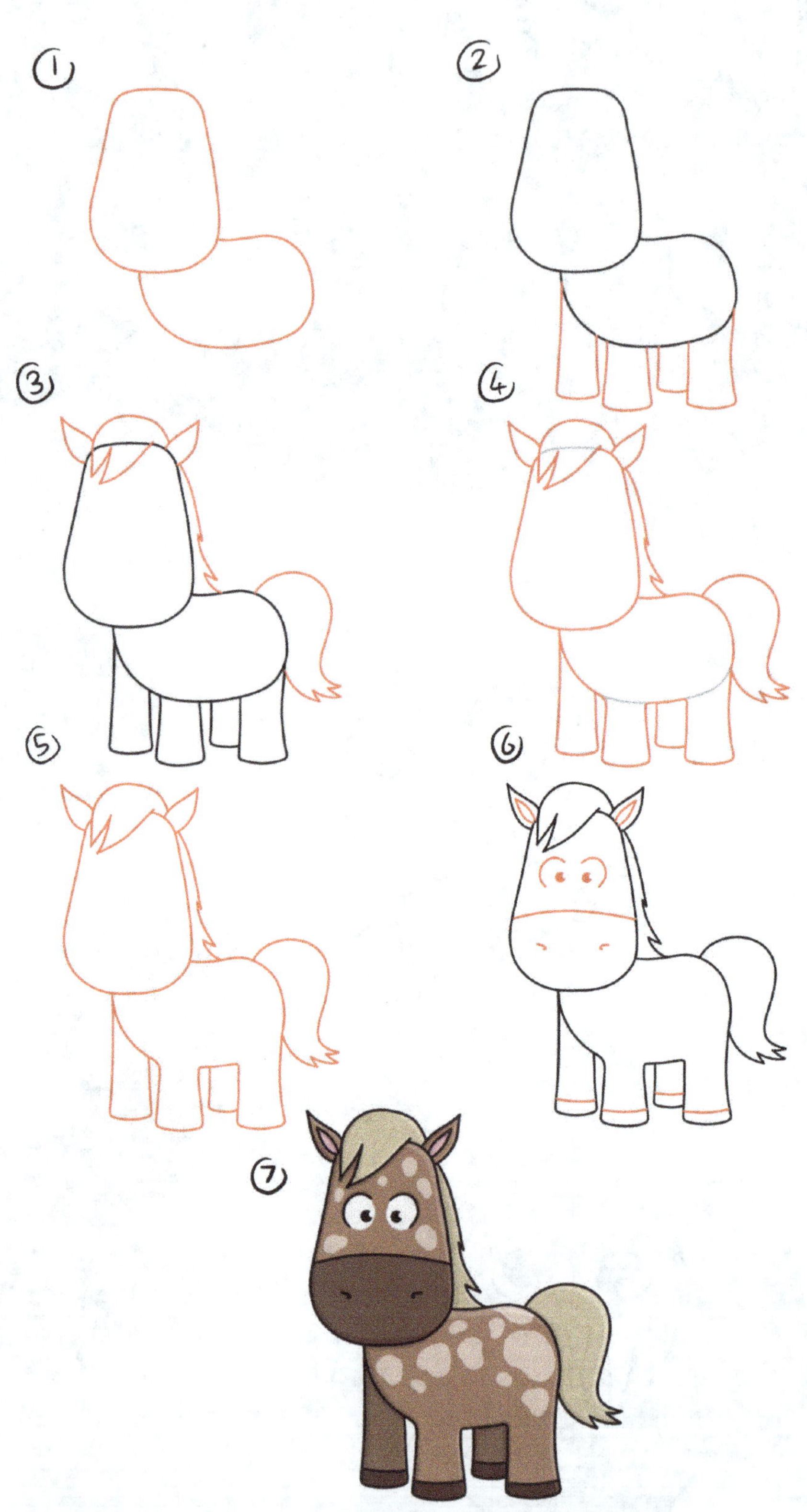

JELLYFISH

 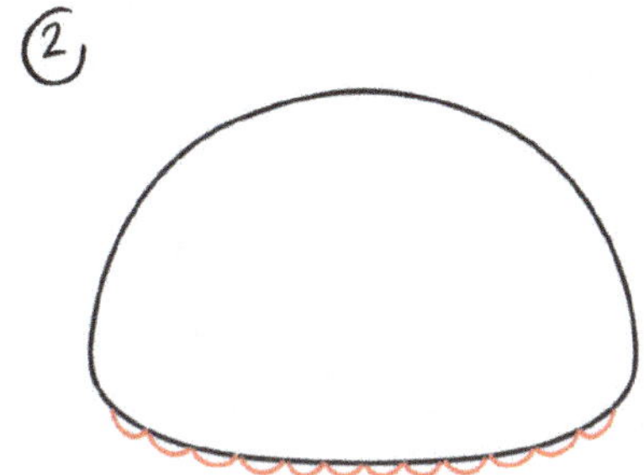

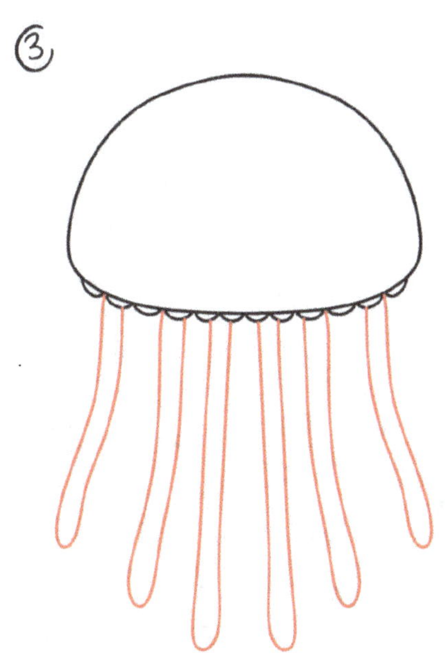 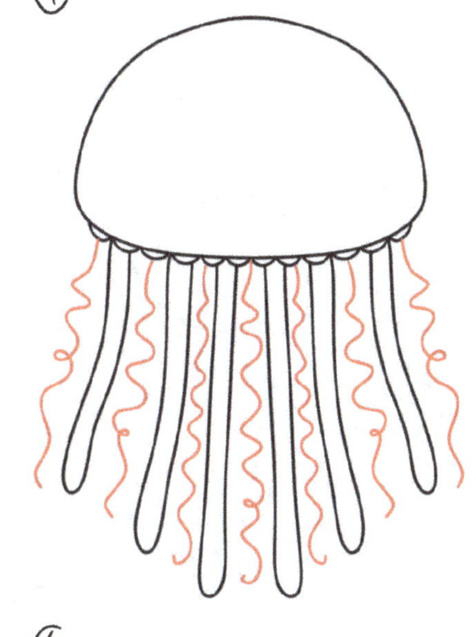

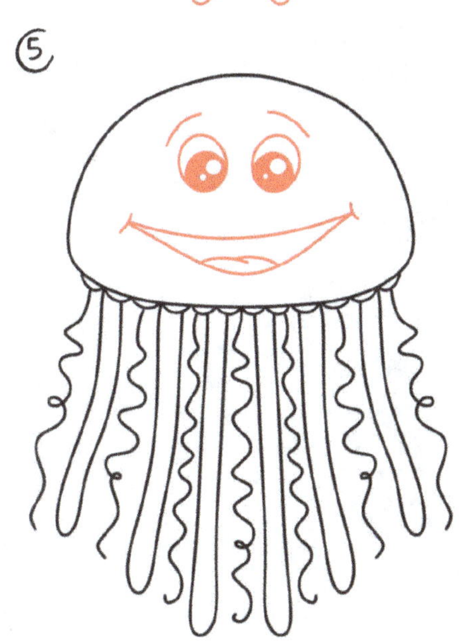 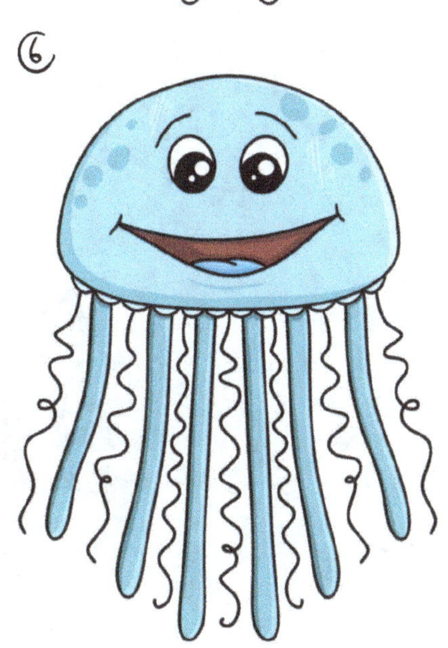

SQUIRREL

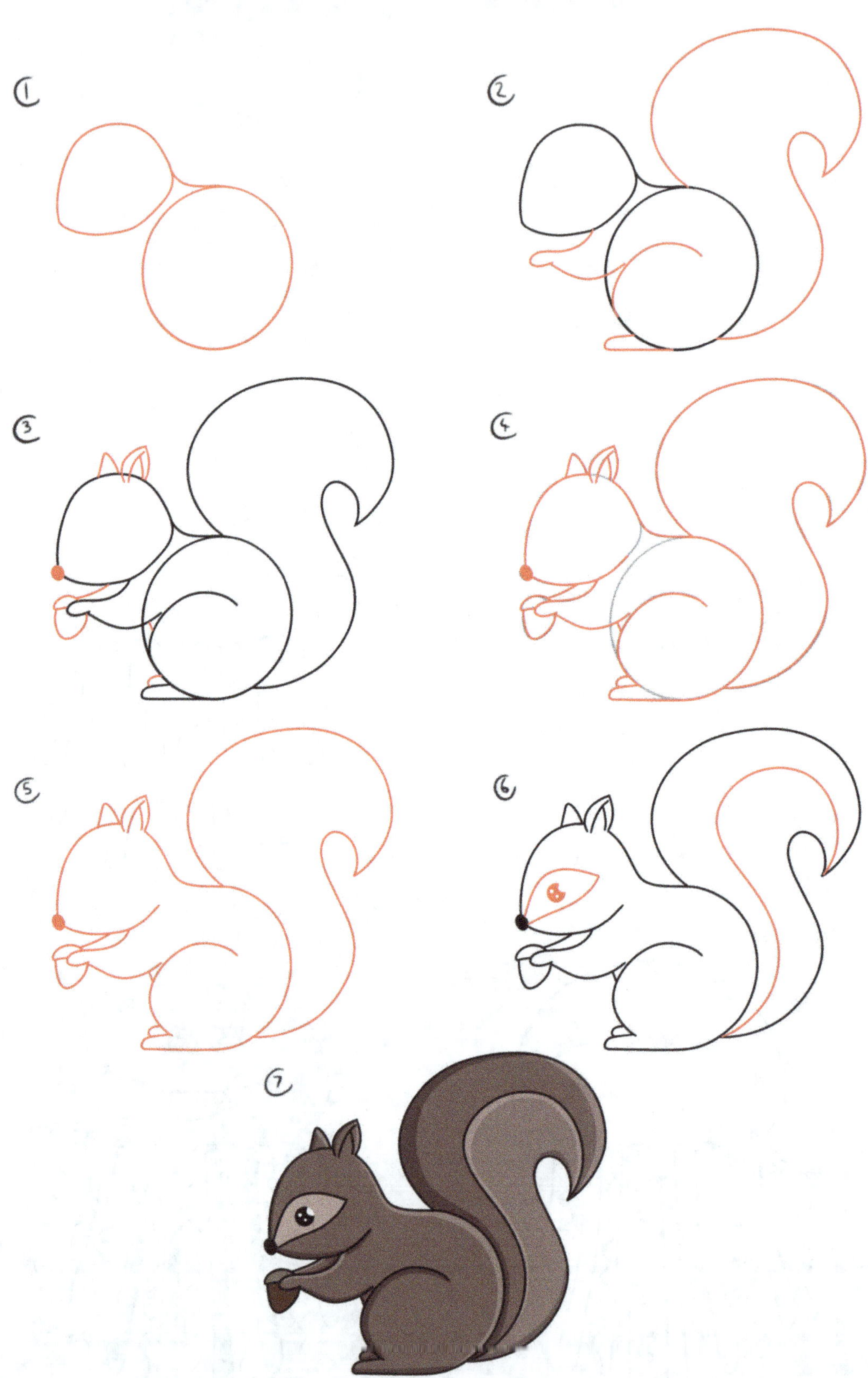

KANGAROO

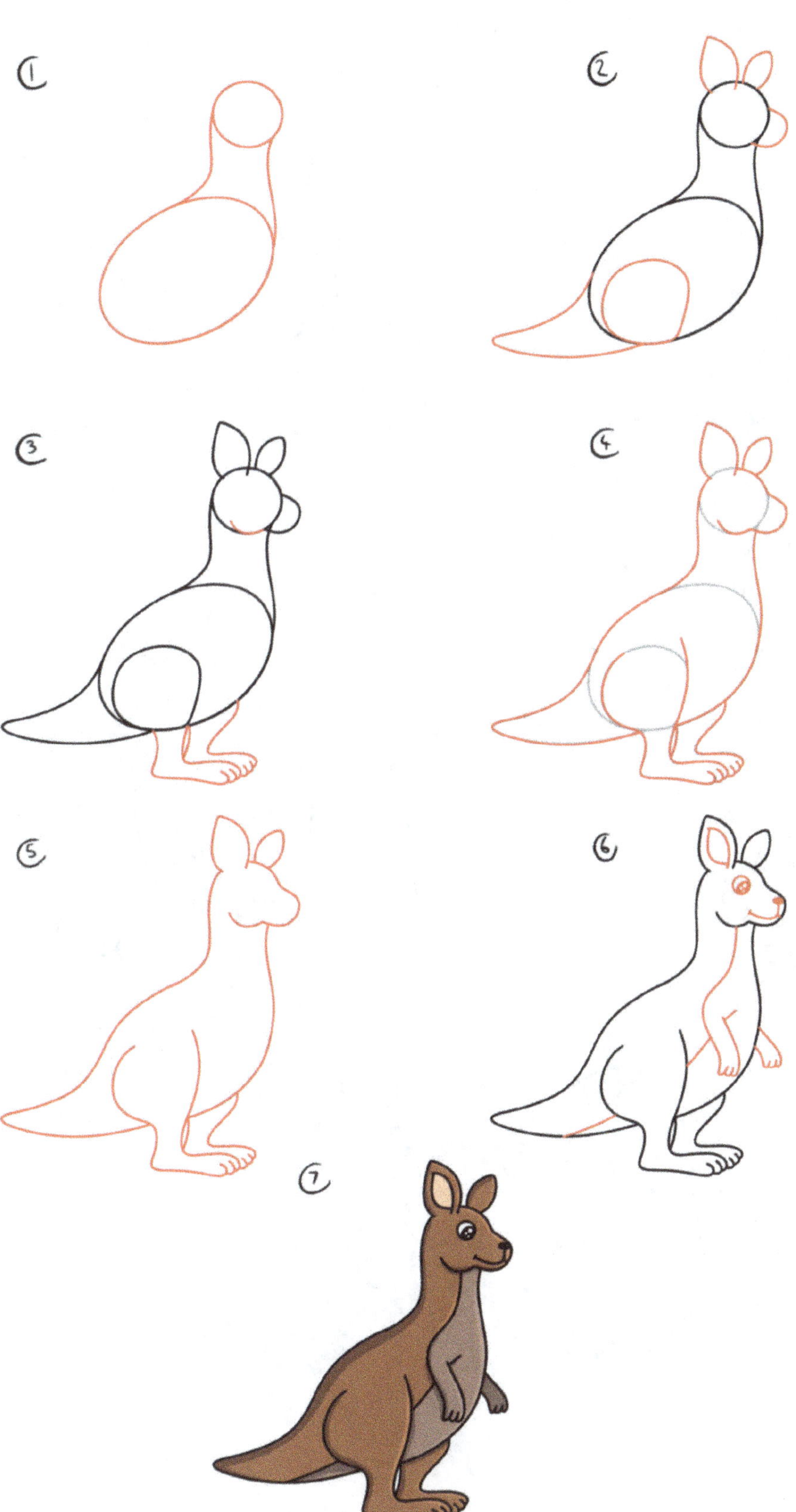

ELEPHANT

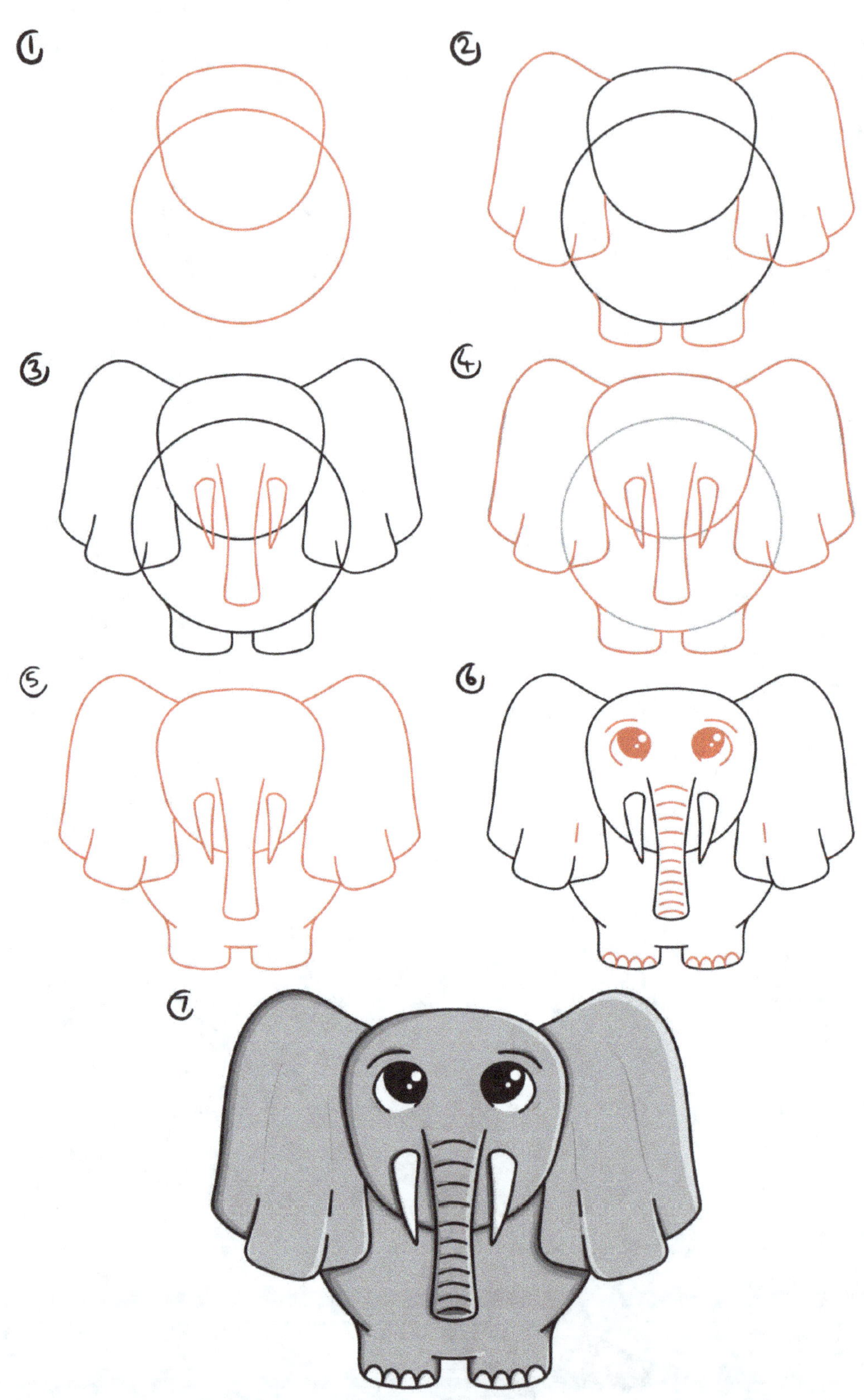

FROG

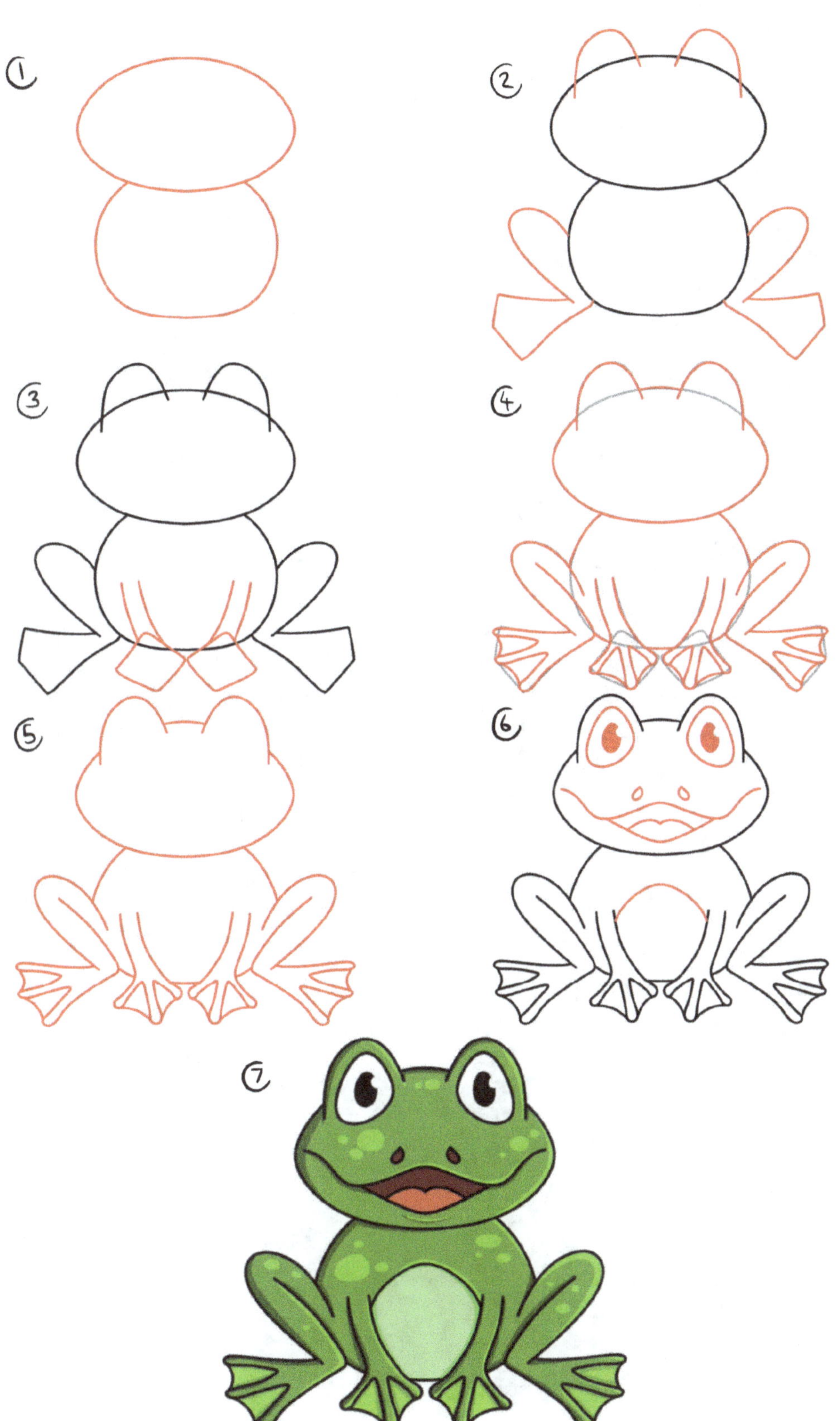

RACCOON

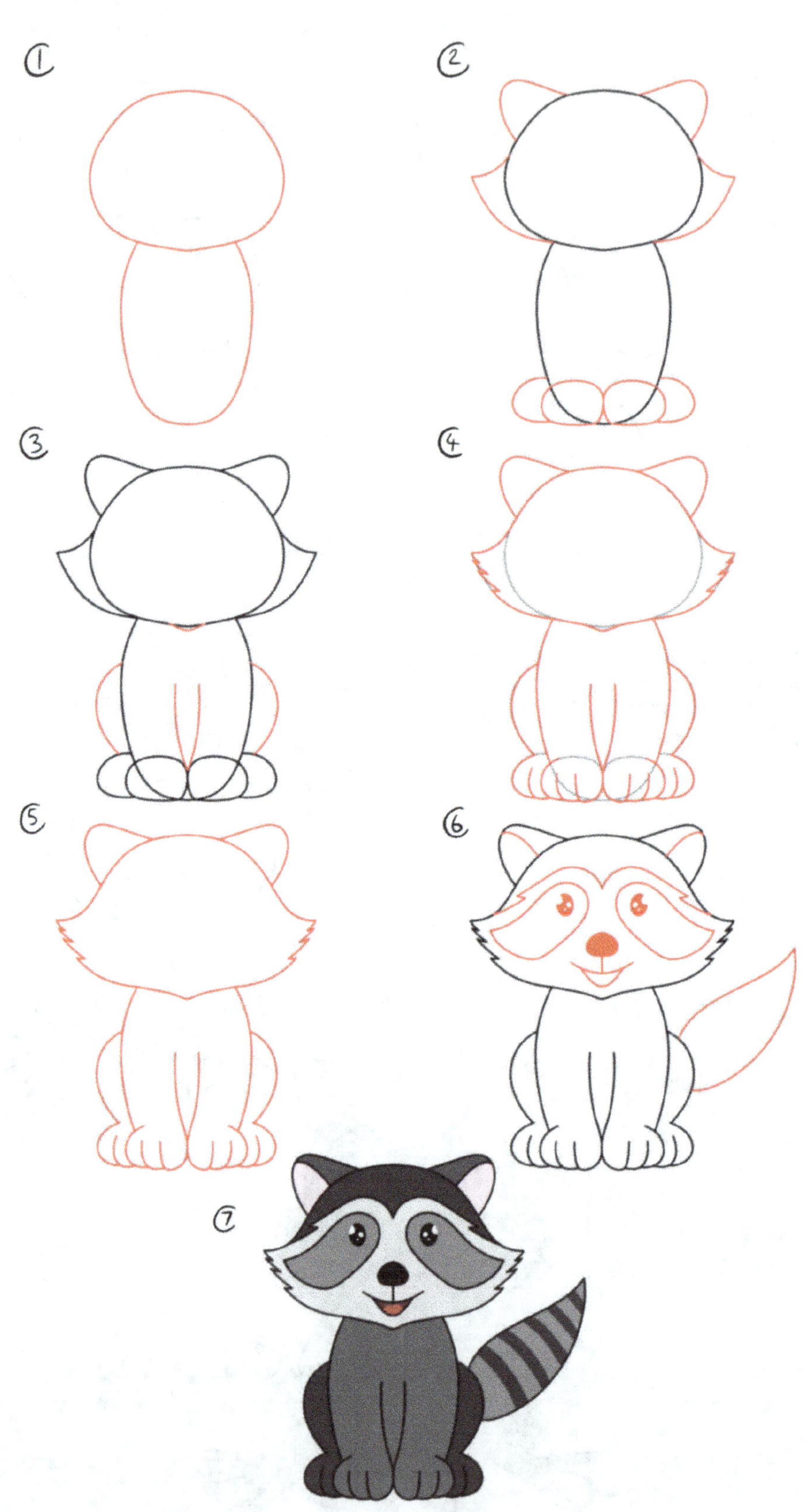

LION

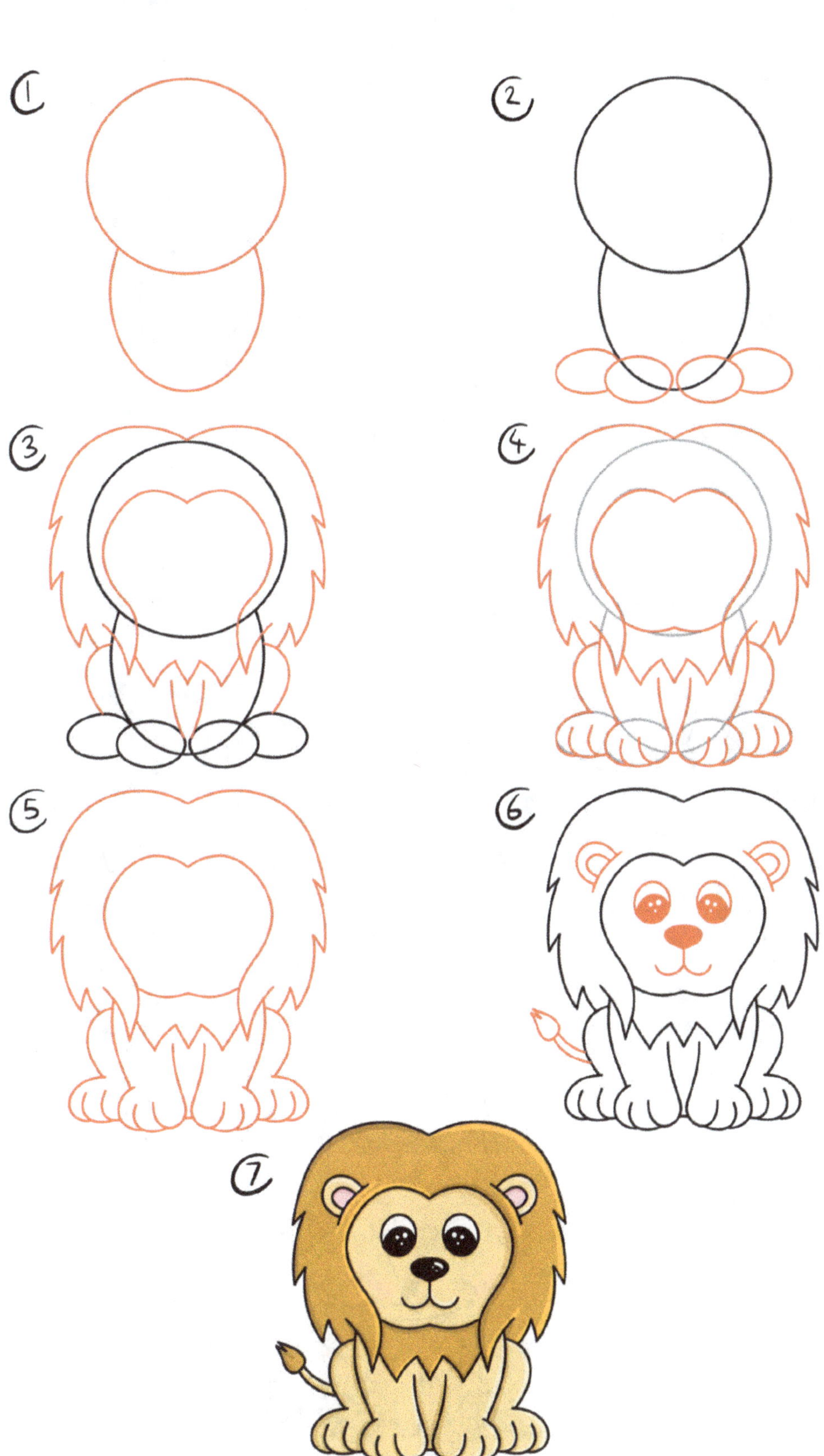

FOX

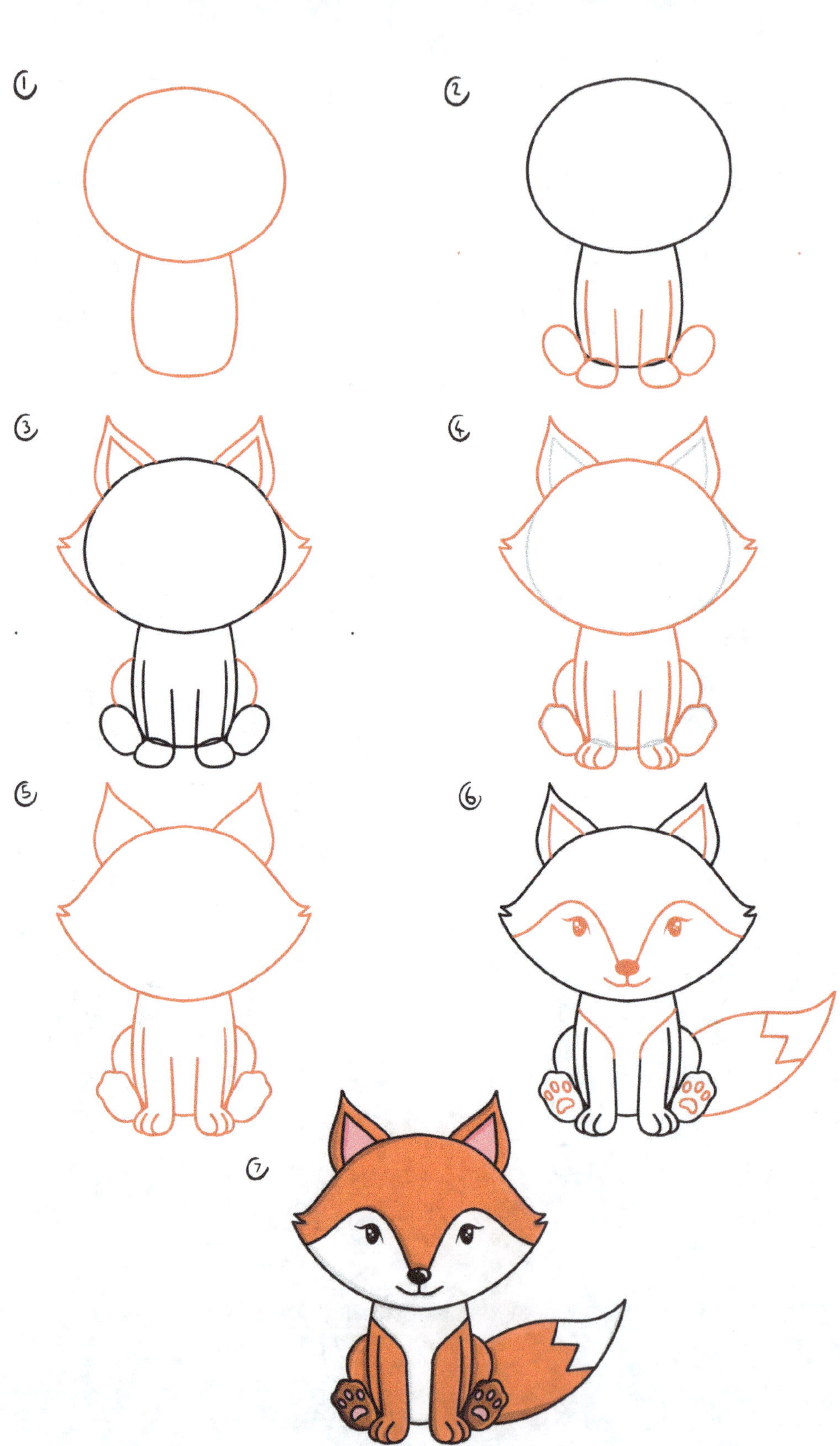

BUTTERFLY

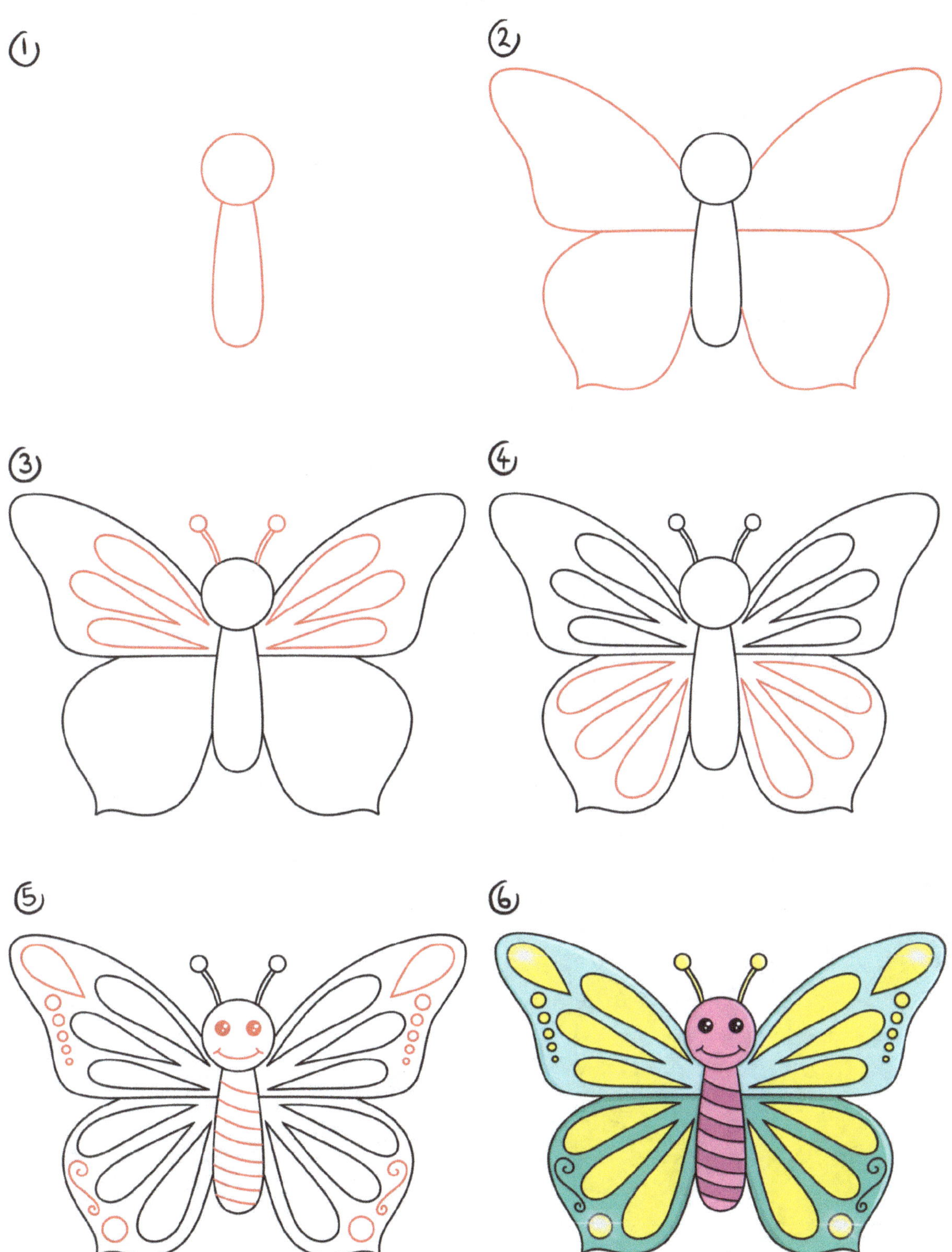

BUNNY

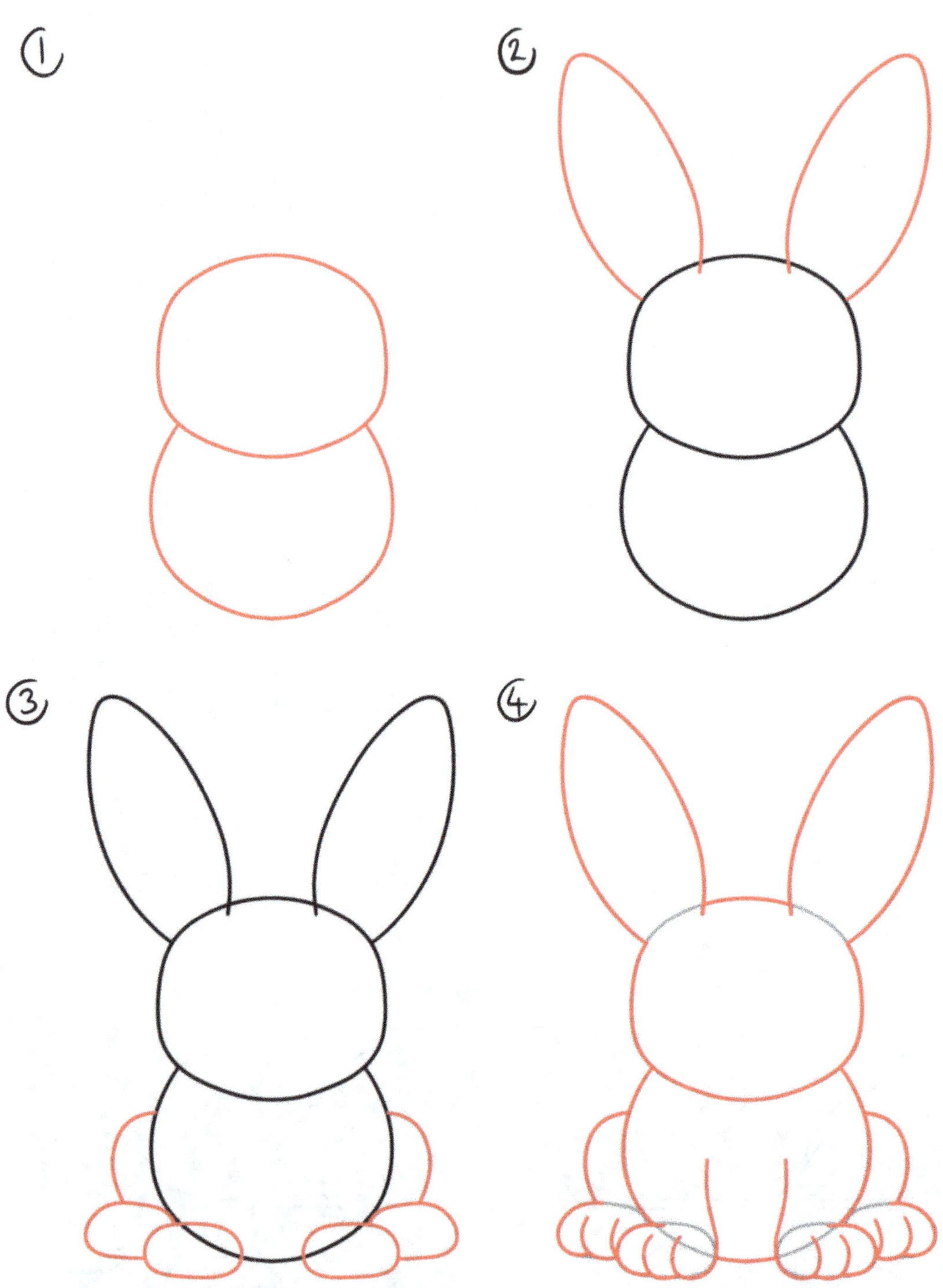

BUNNY

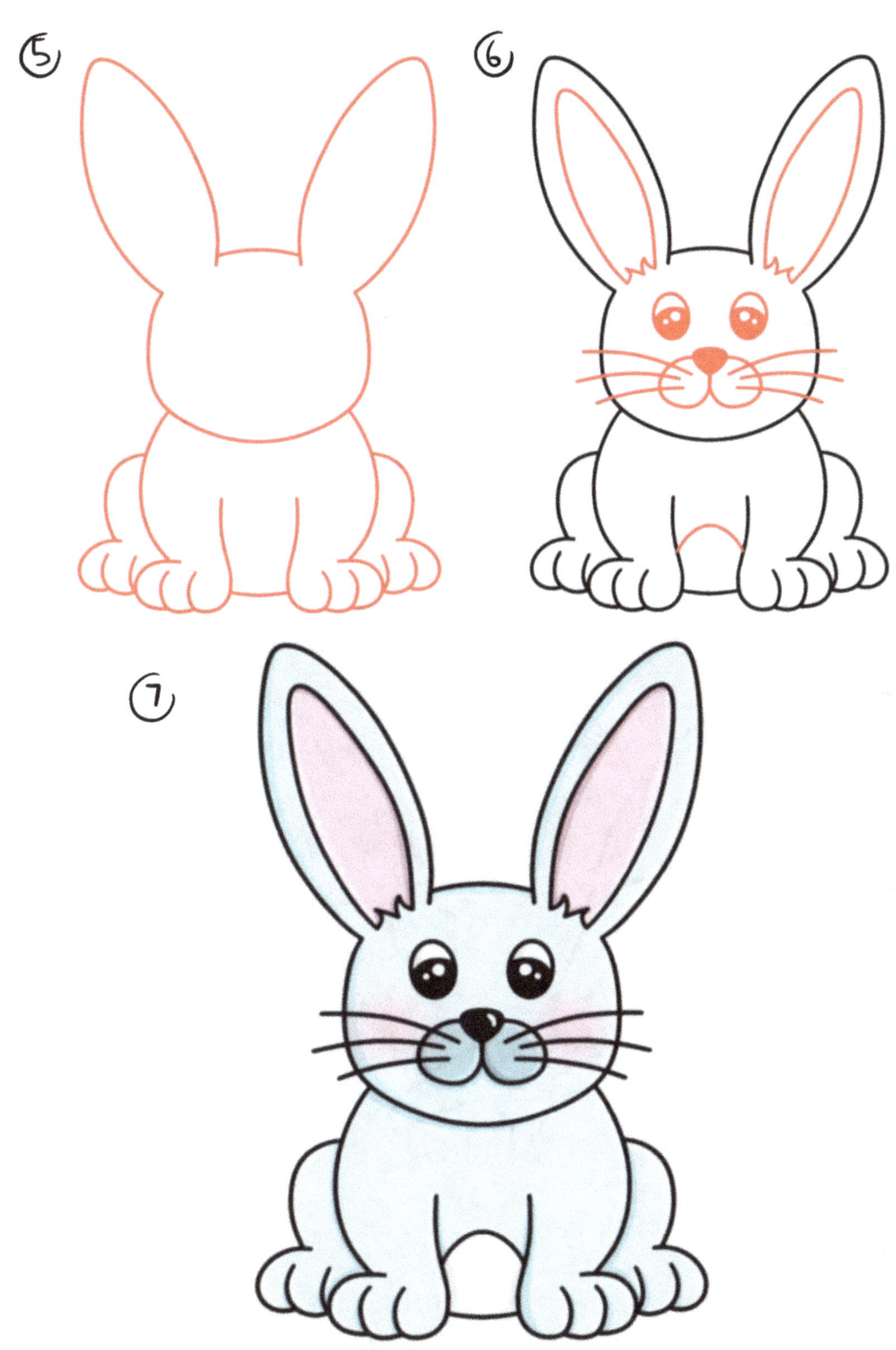

DOLPHIN

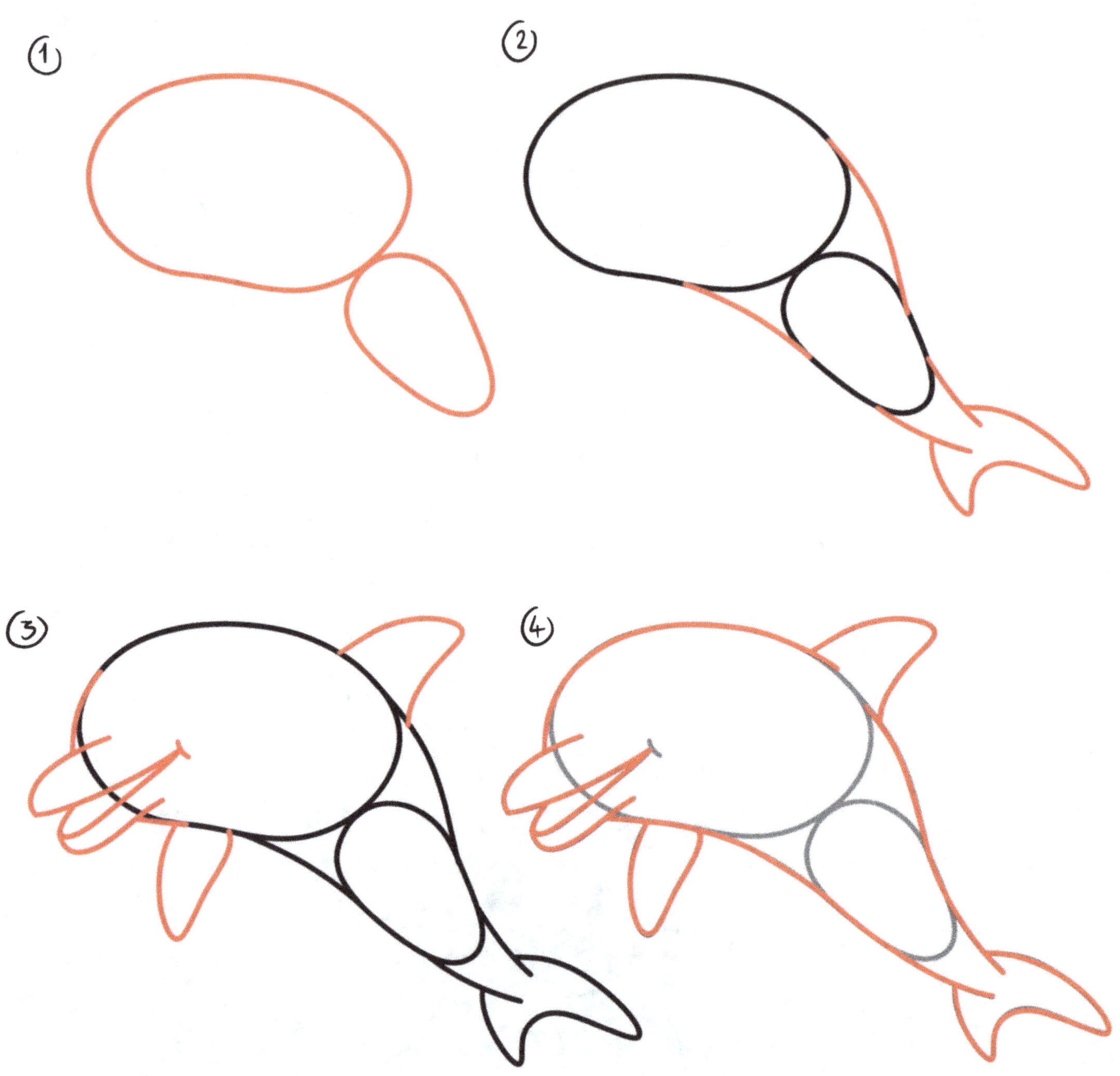

DOLPHIN

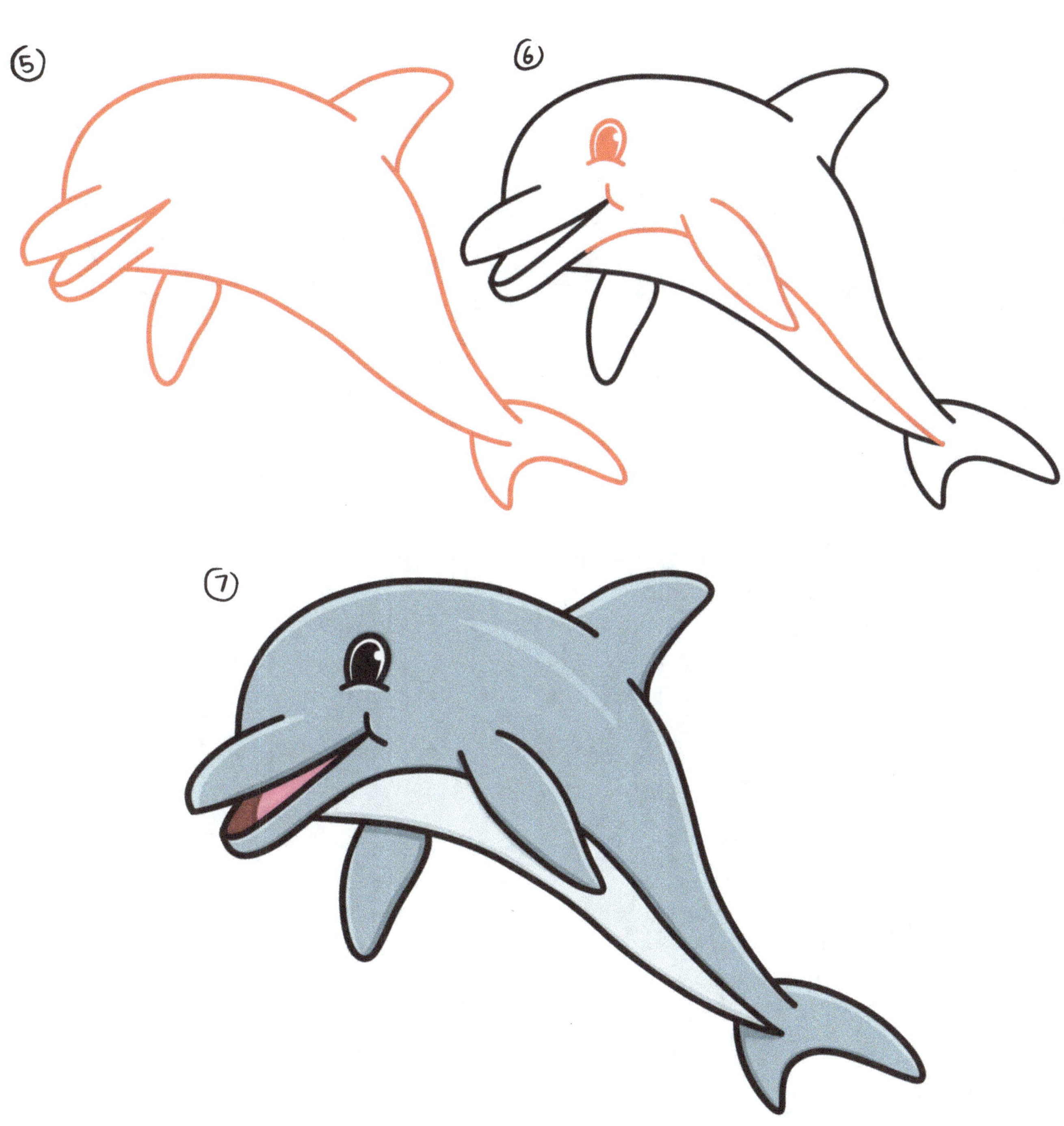

HIPPO

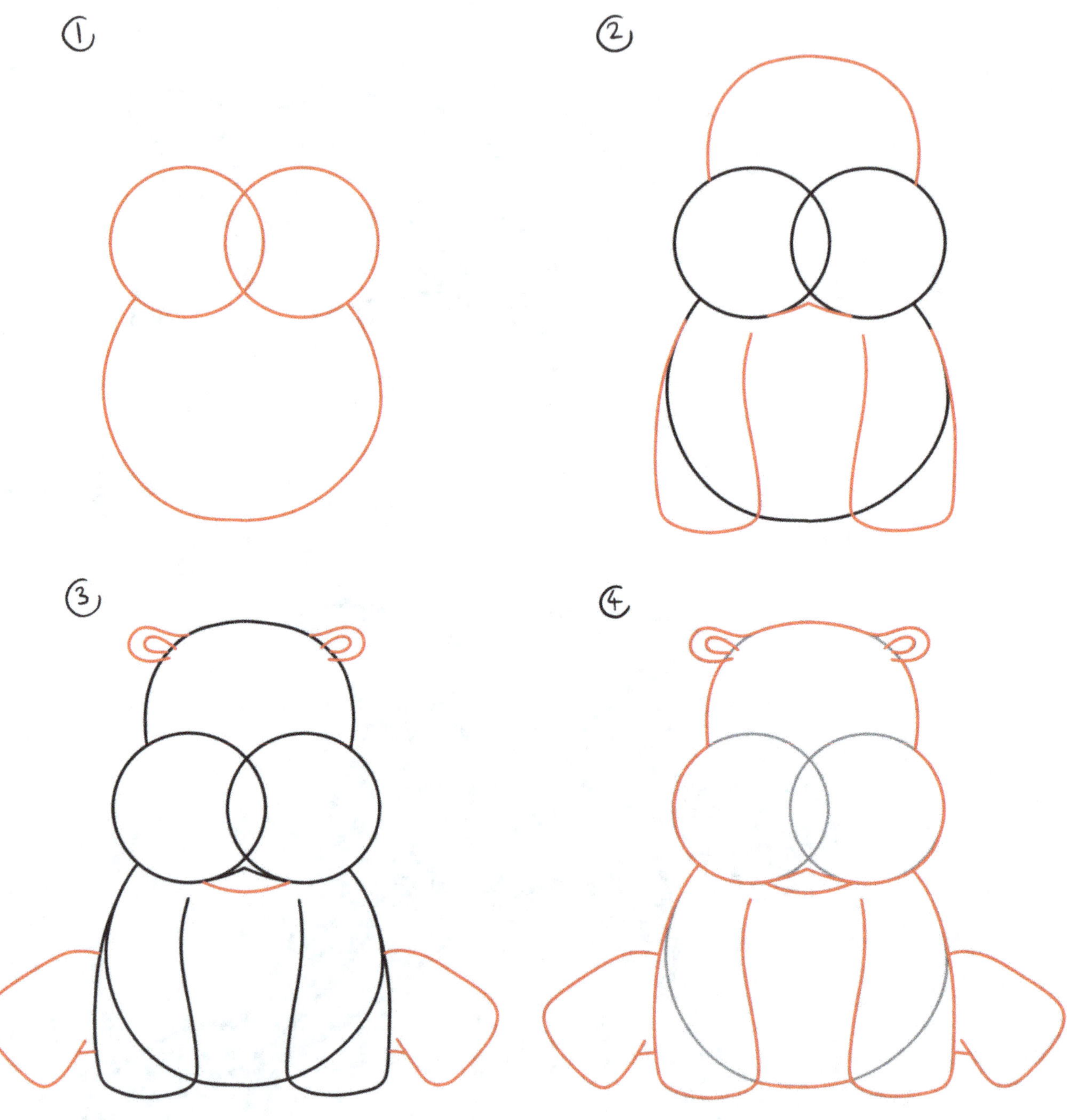

HIPPO

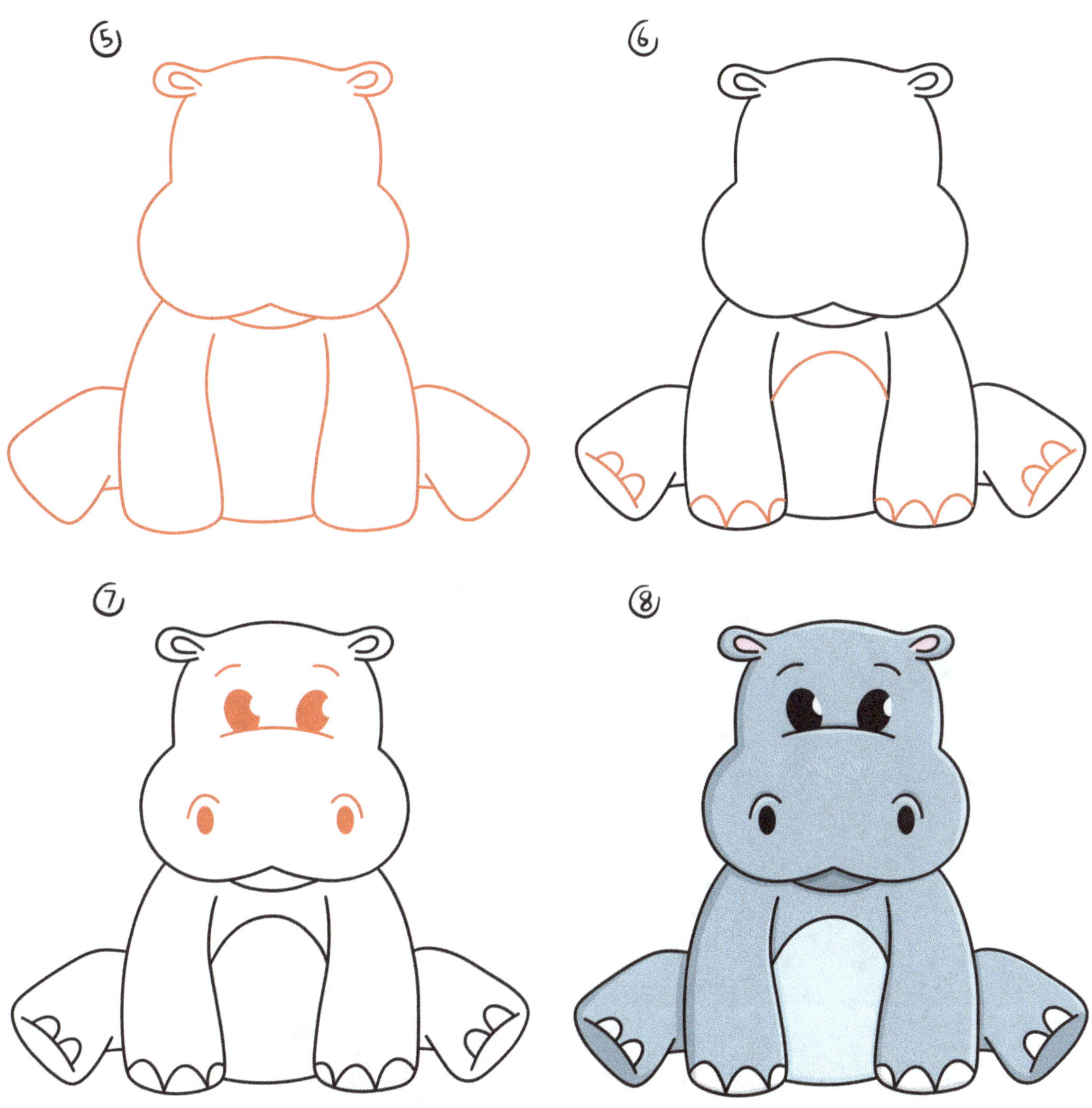

PANDA

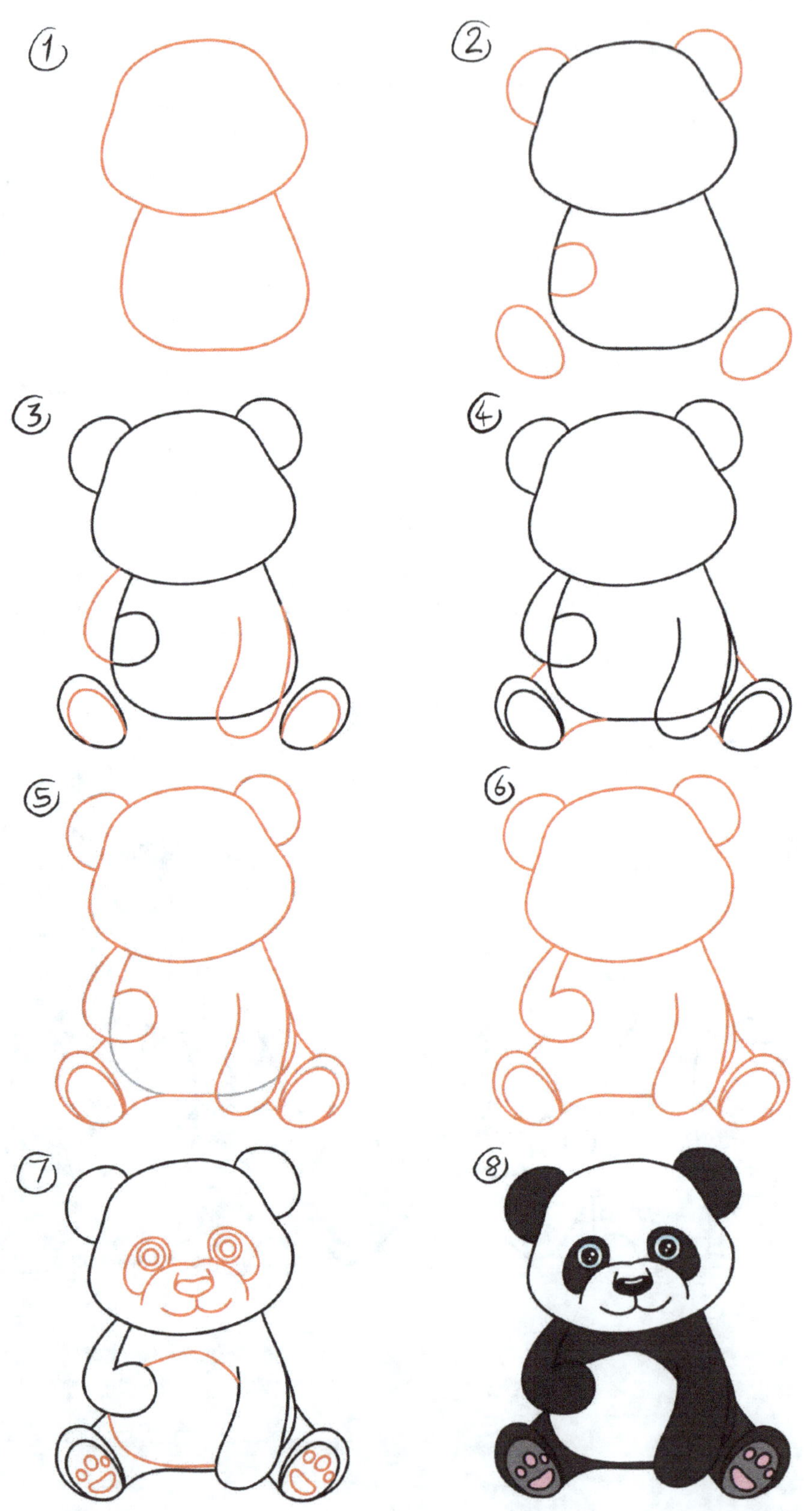

TIGER

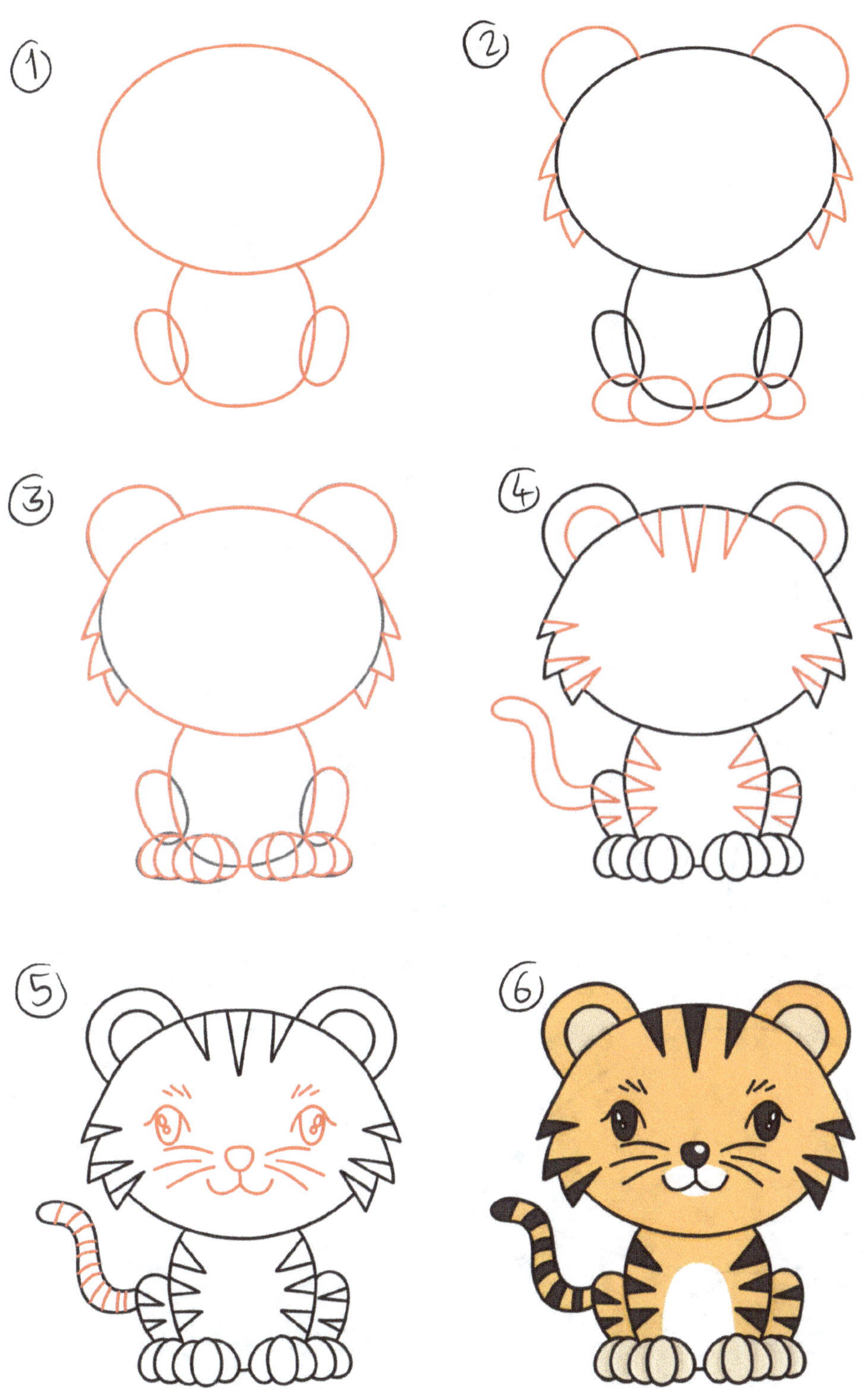

DUCK

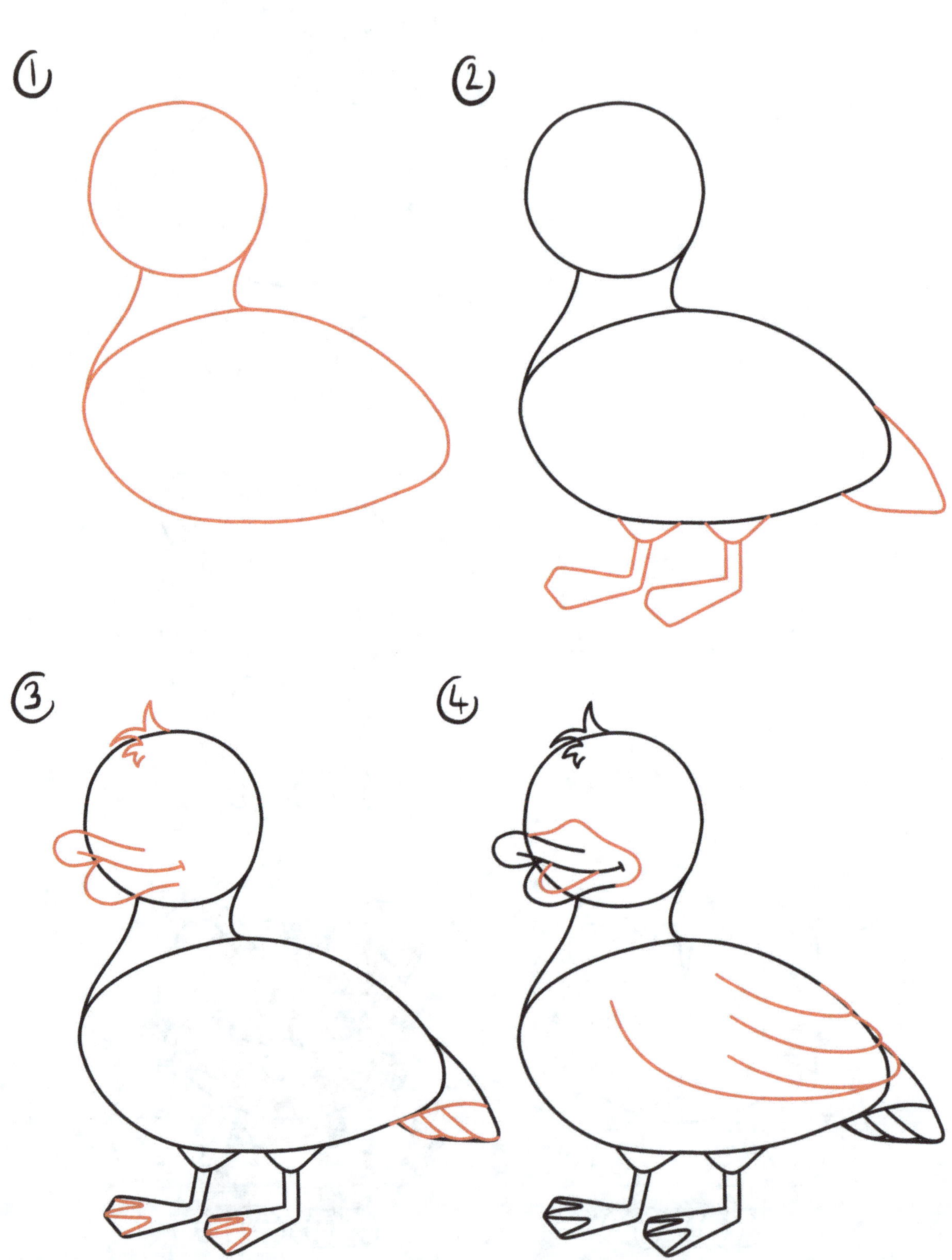

DUCK

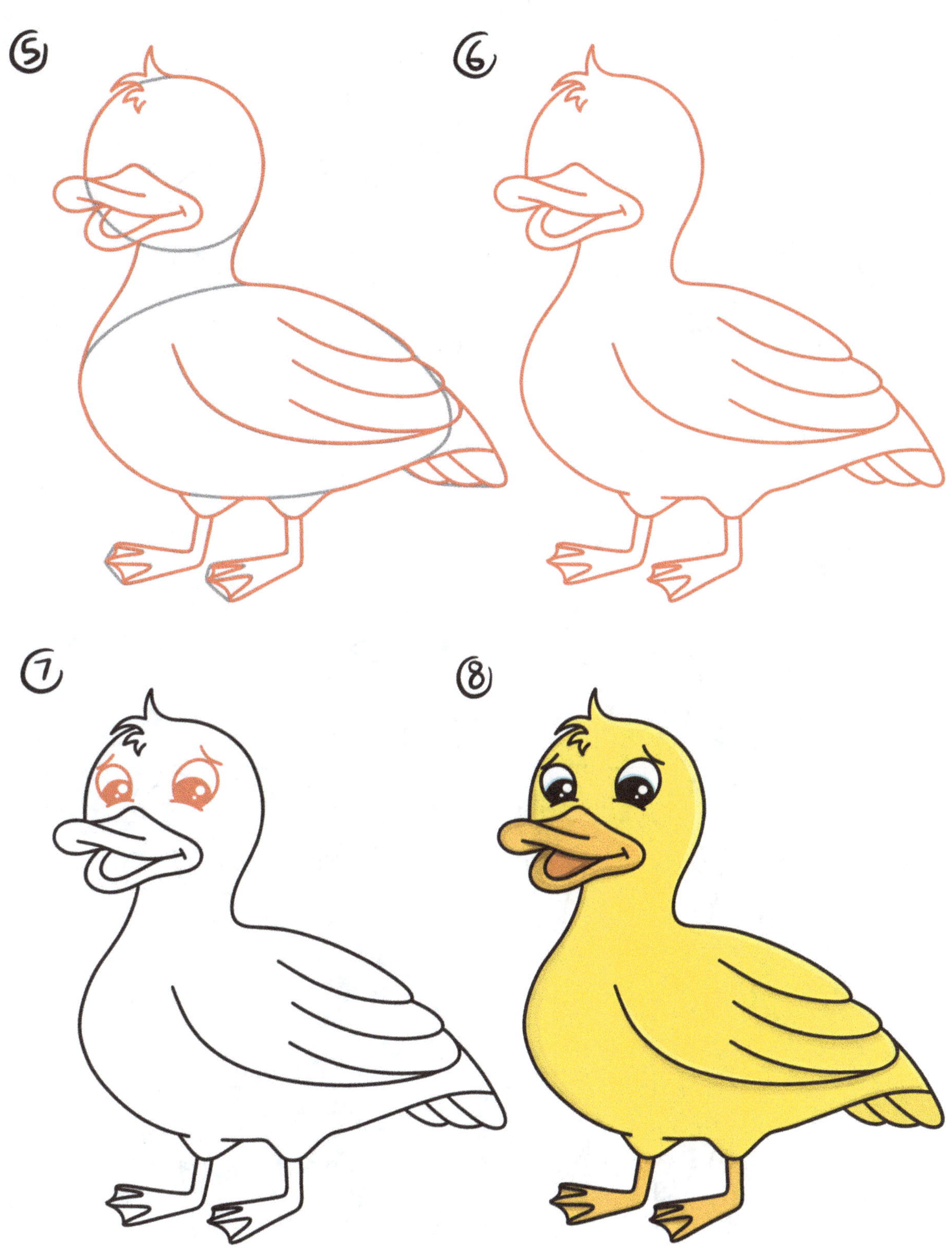

ZEBRA

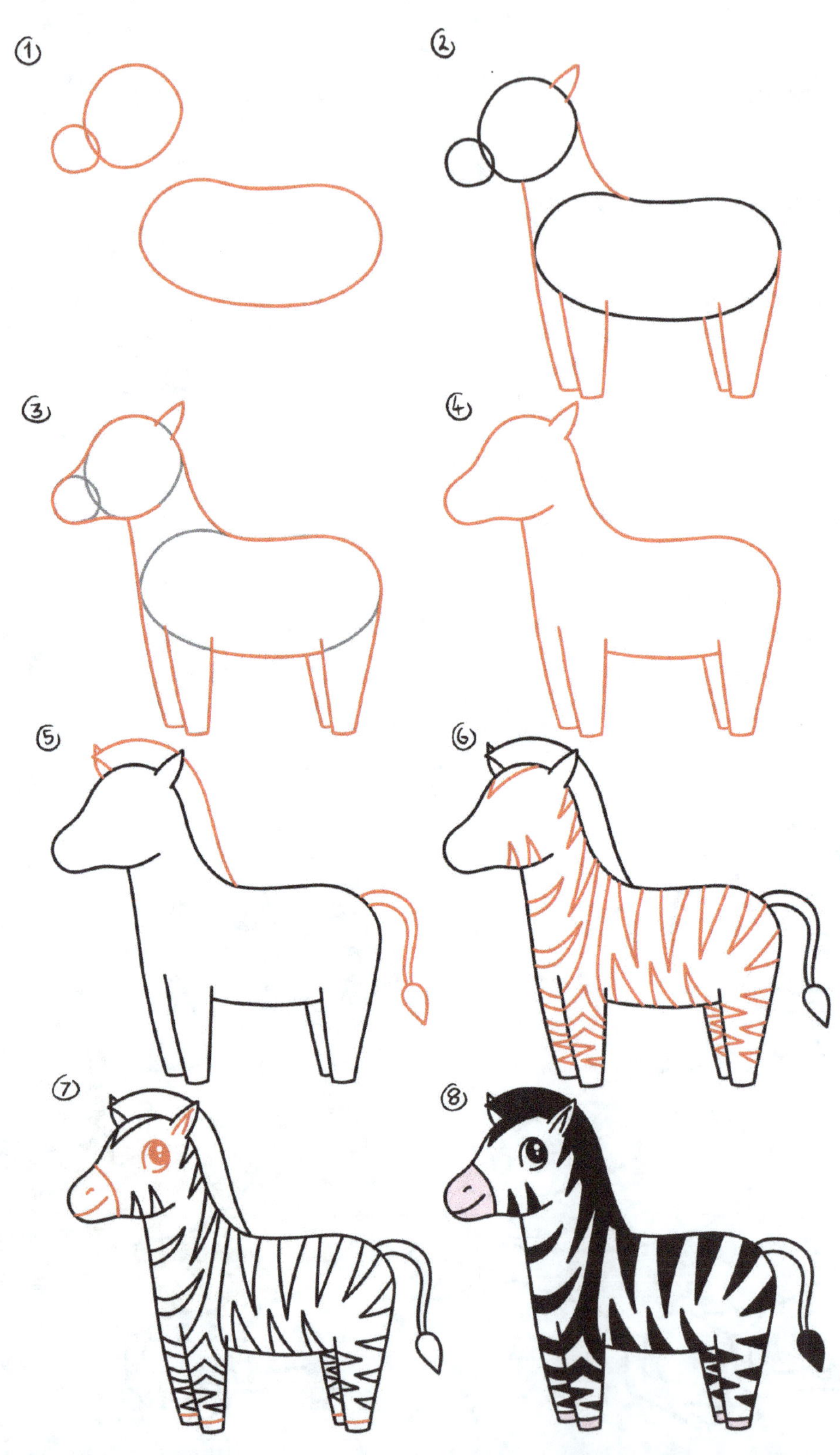

COMPLEX DESIGNS

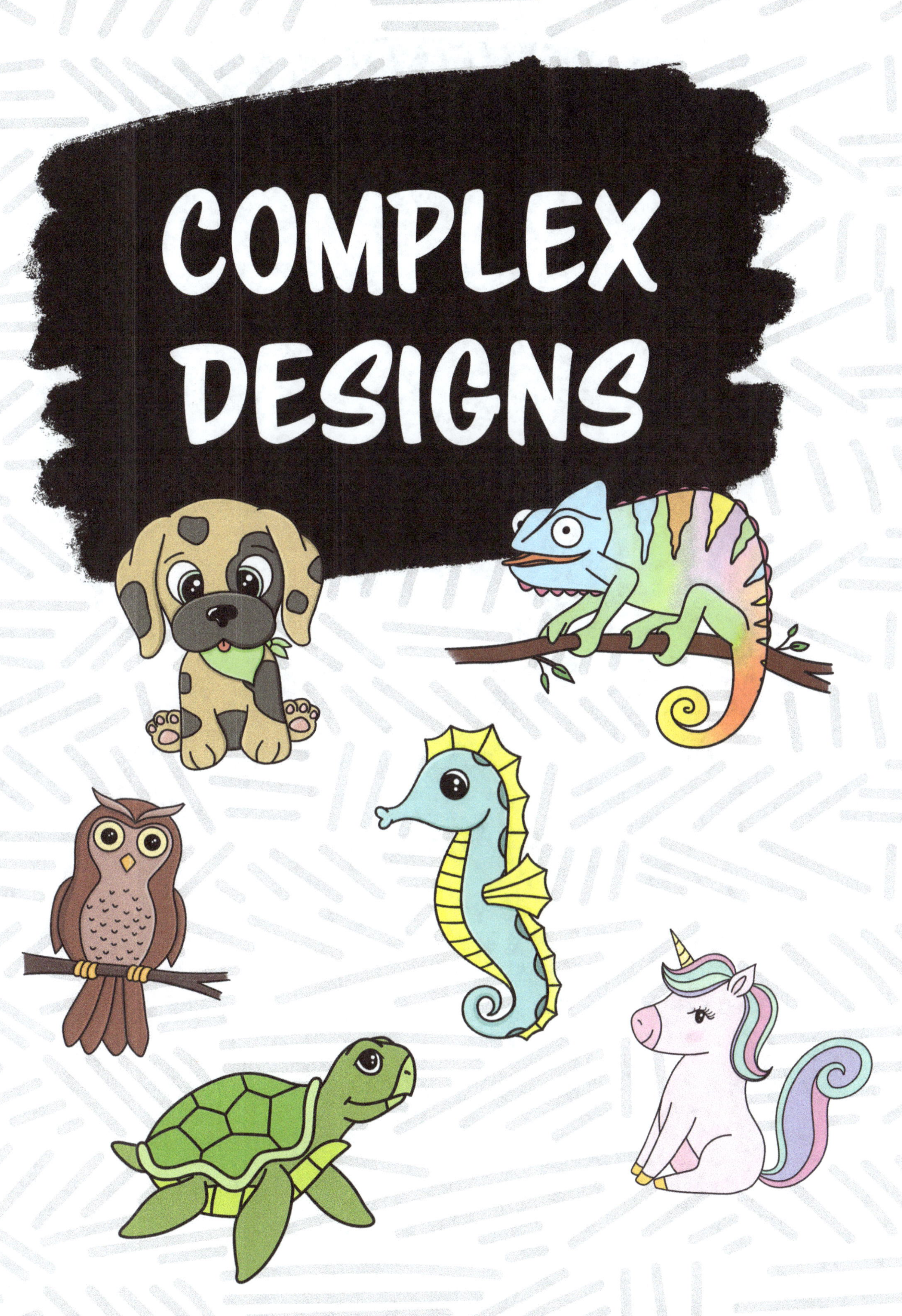

DRAGON

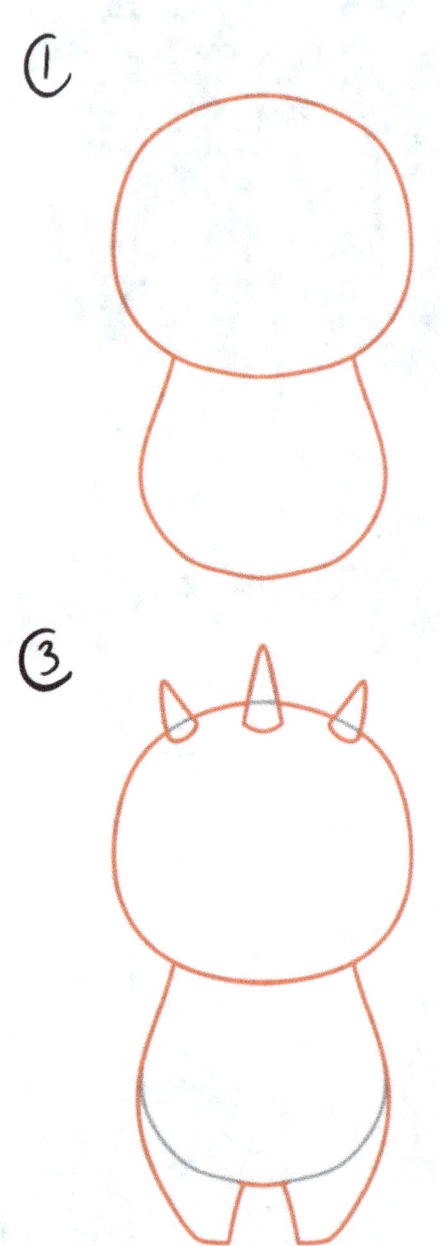

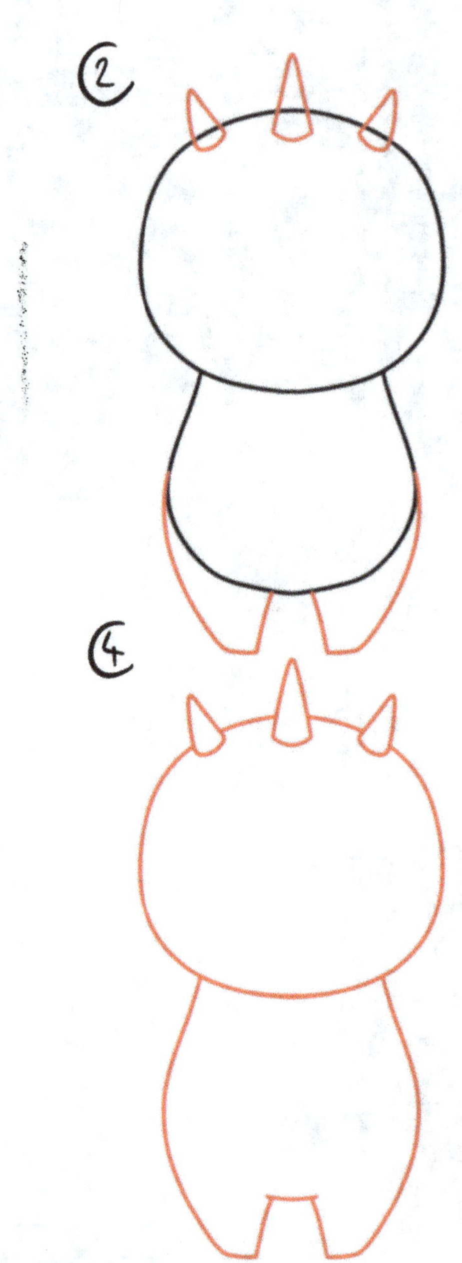

DRAGON

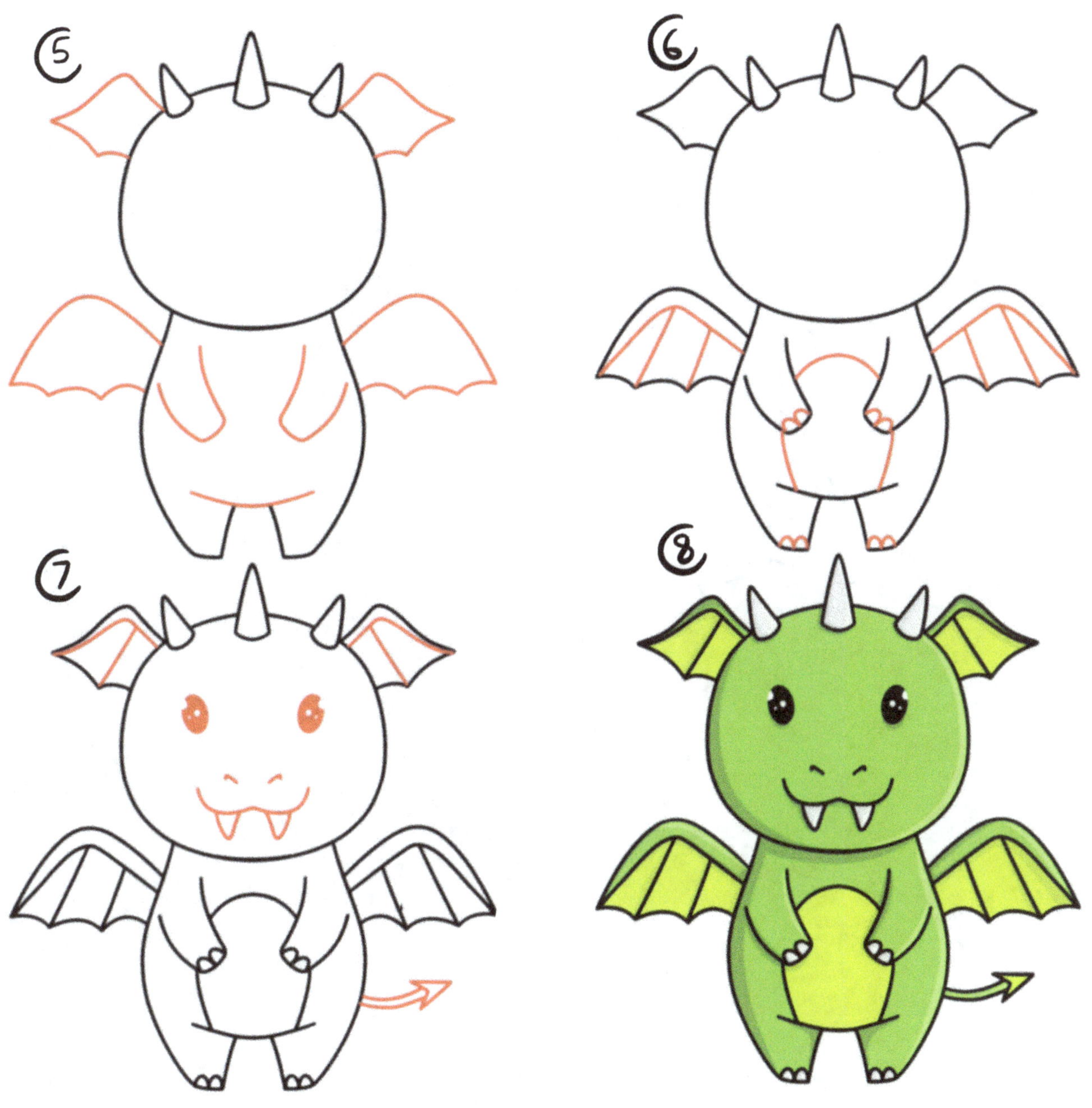

PARROT

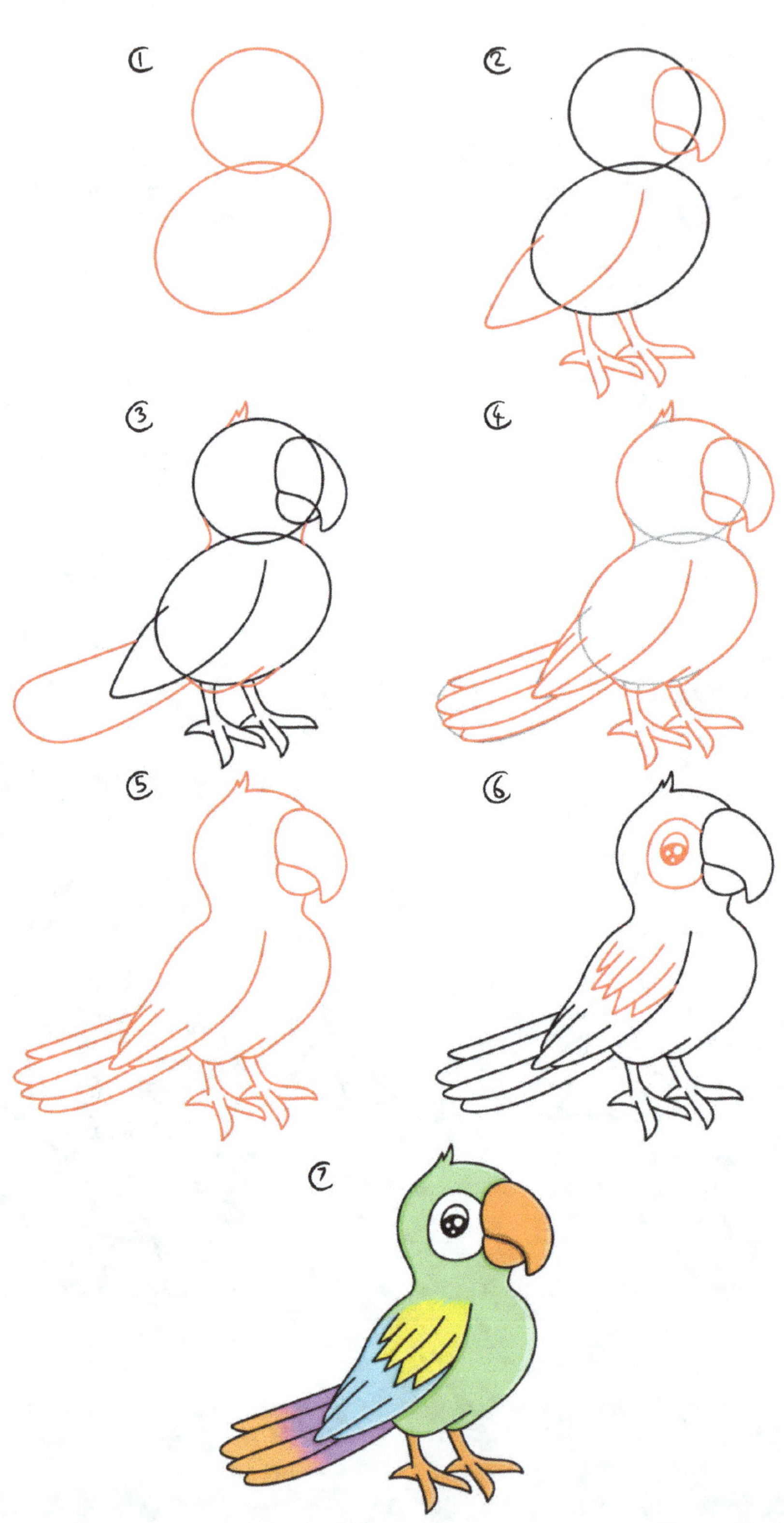

CHEETAH

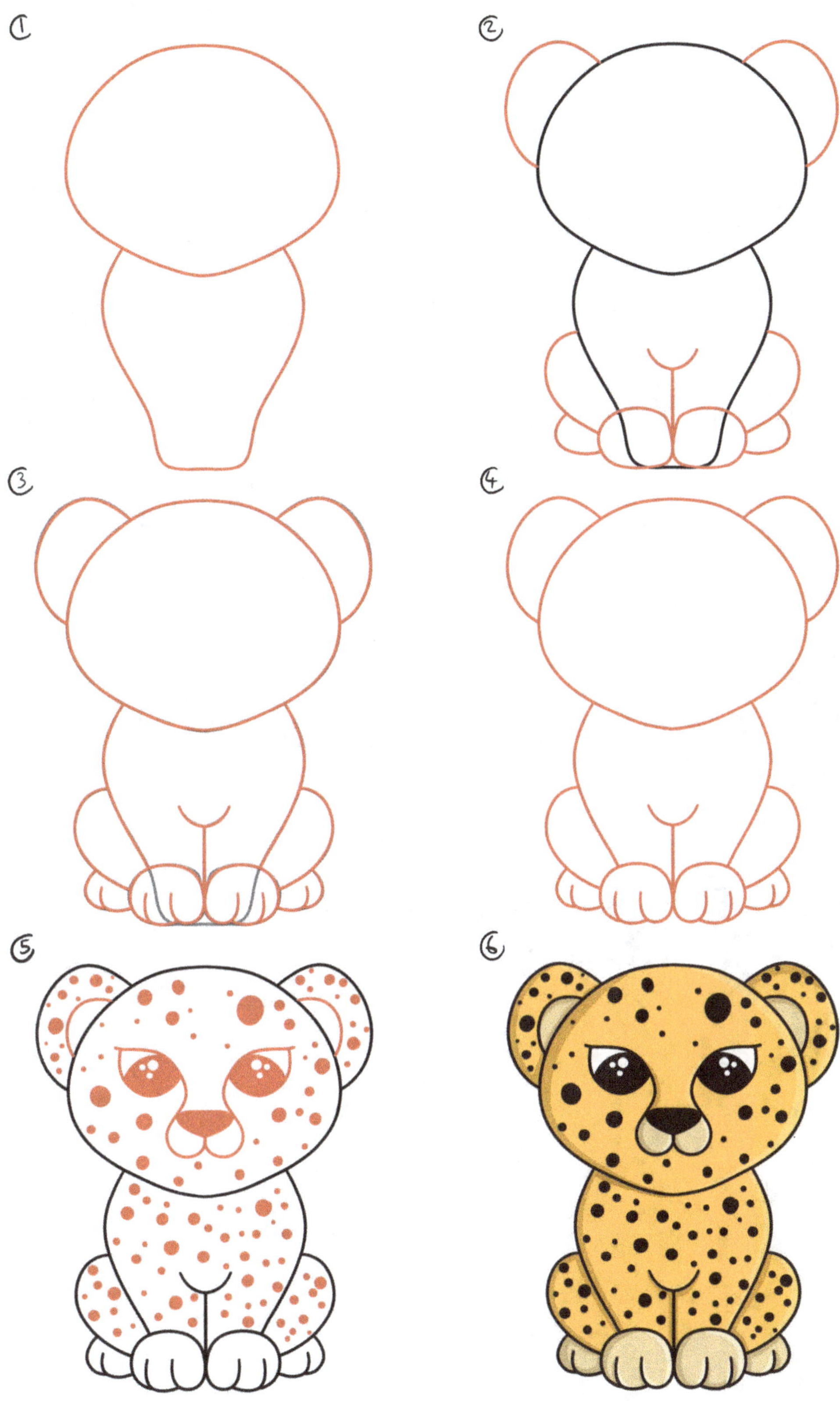

T-REX

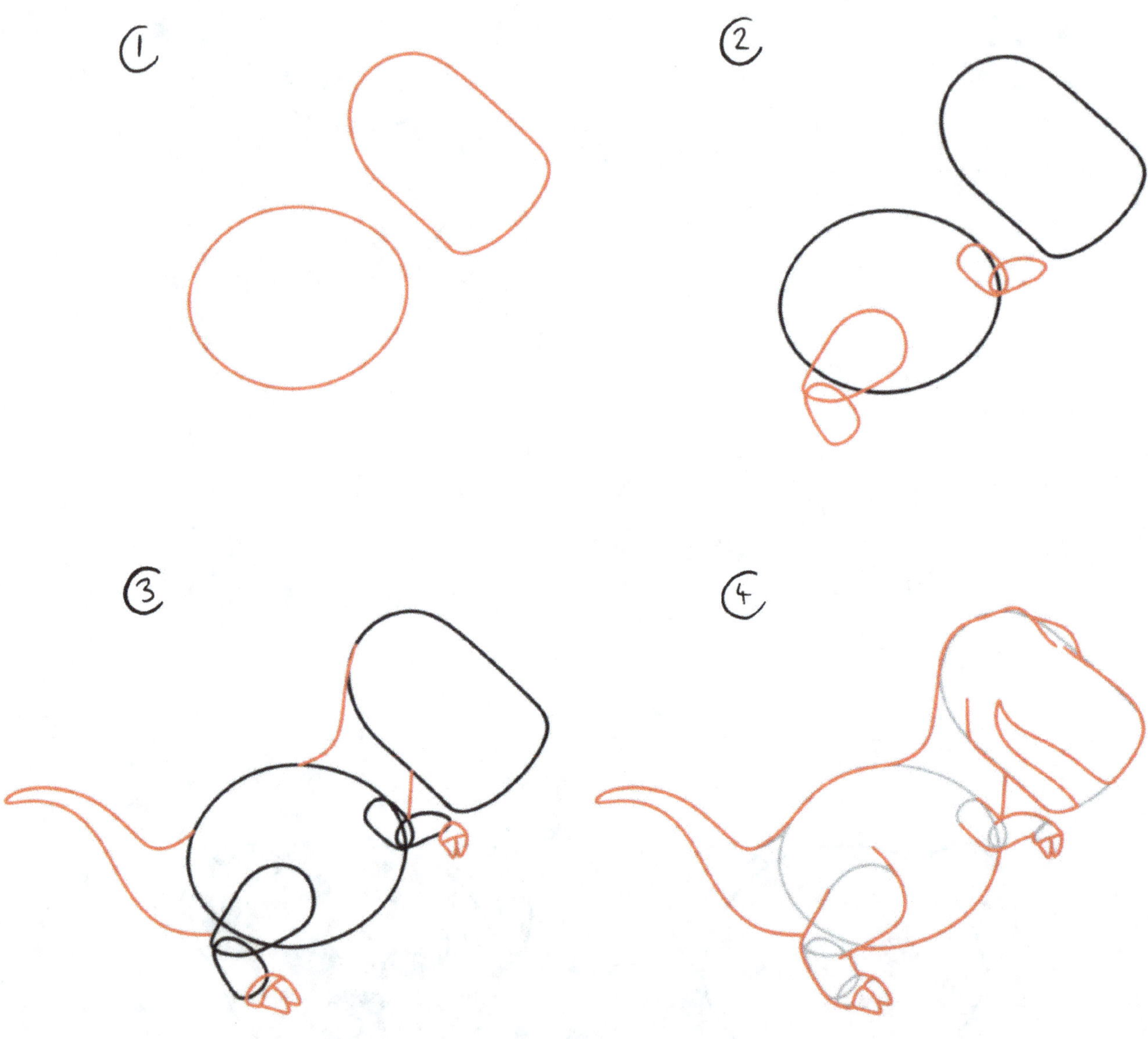

T-REX

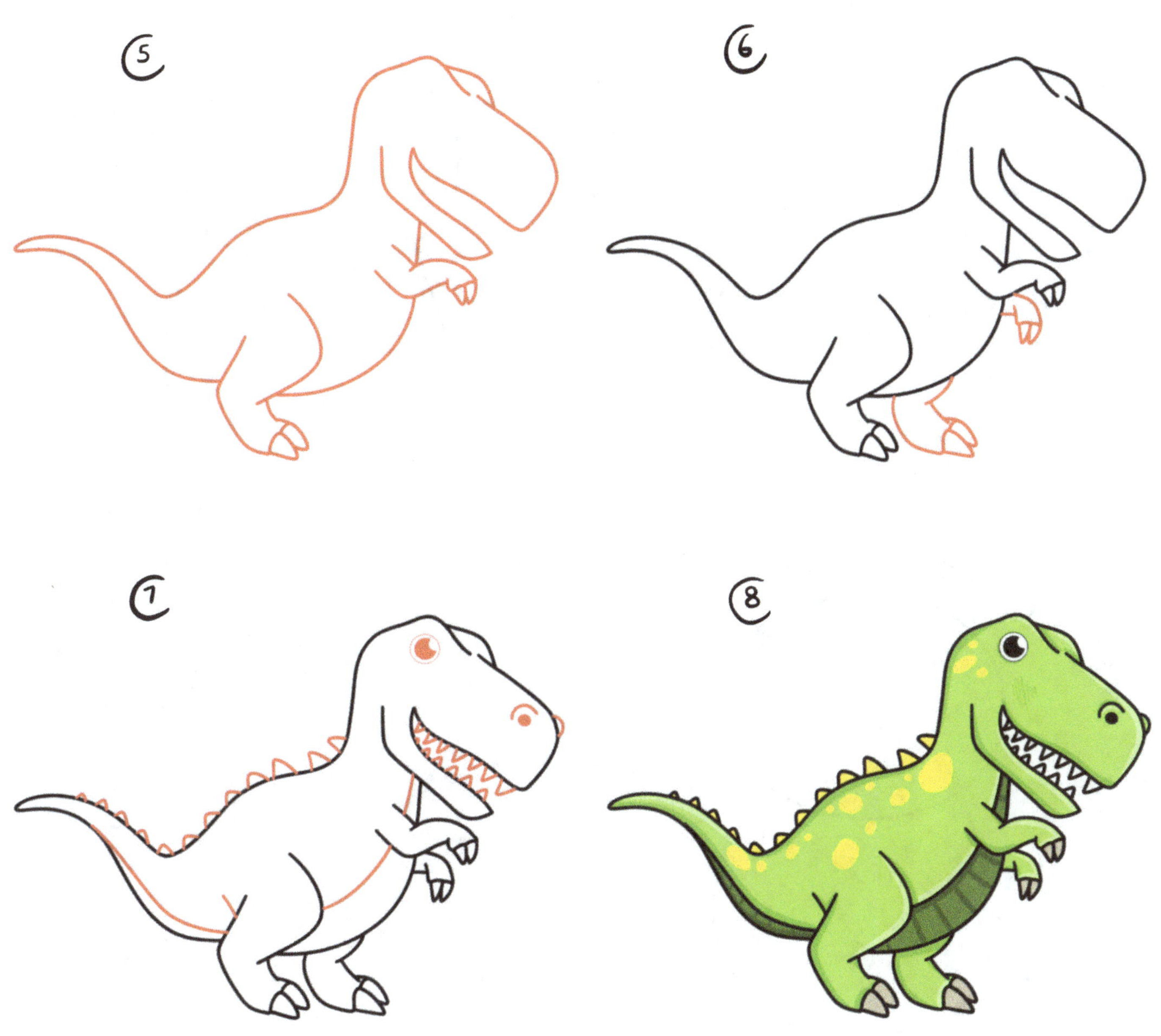

HAMSTER

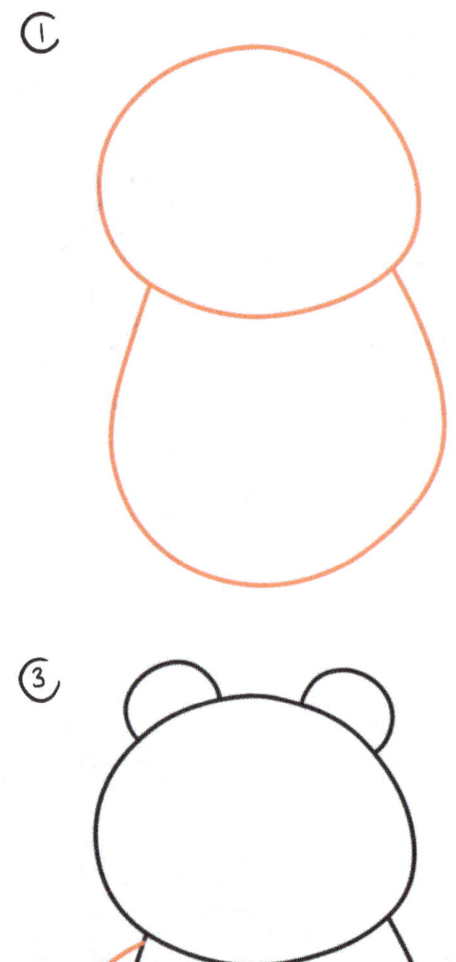

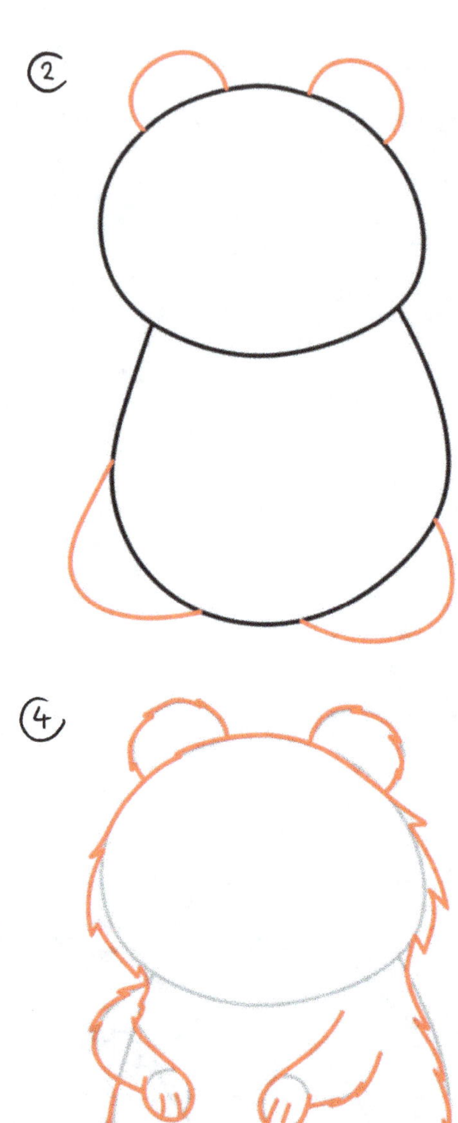

HAMSTER

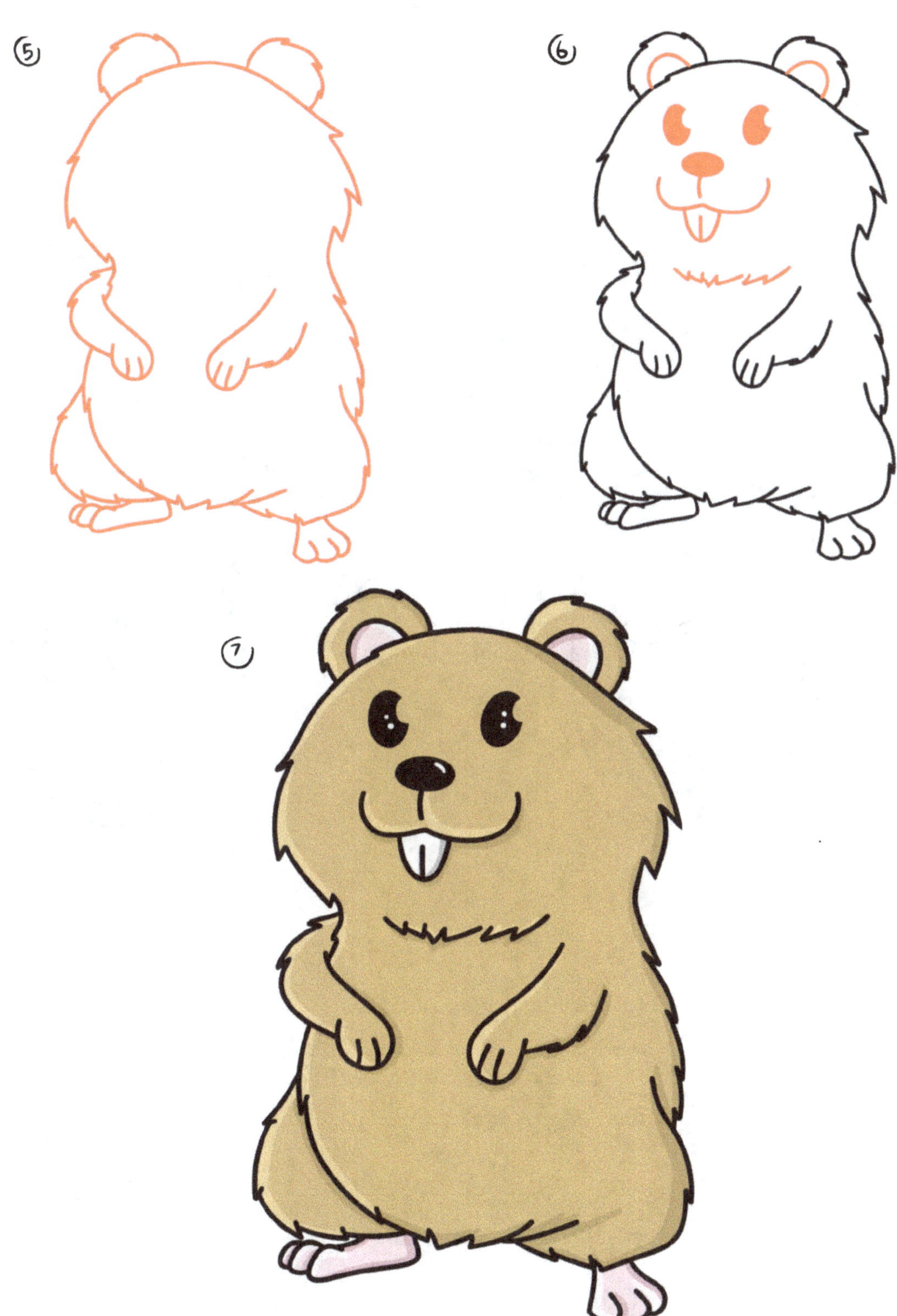

CHAMELEON

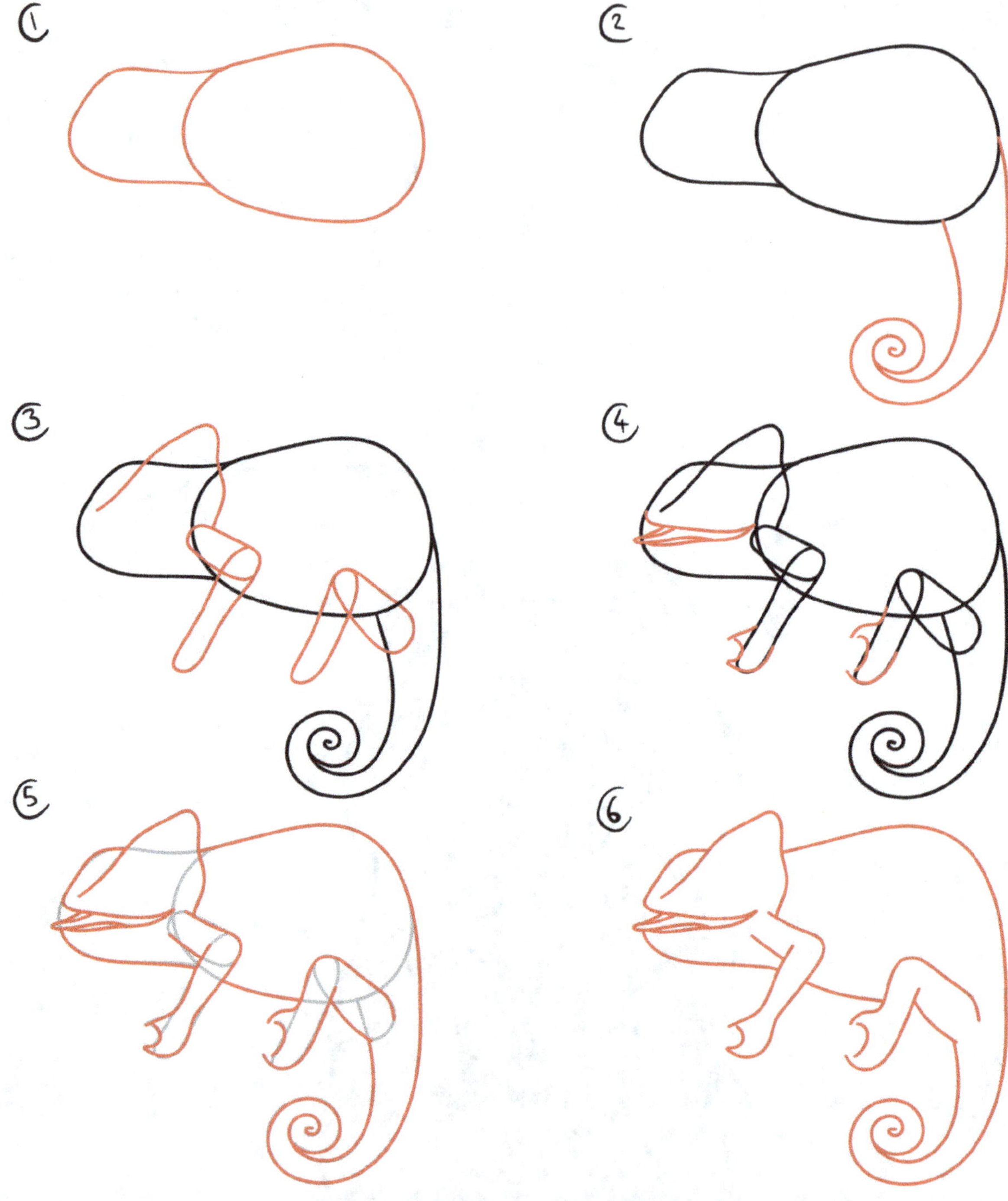

CHAMELEON

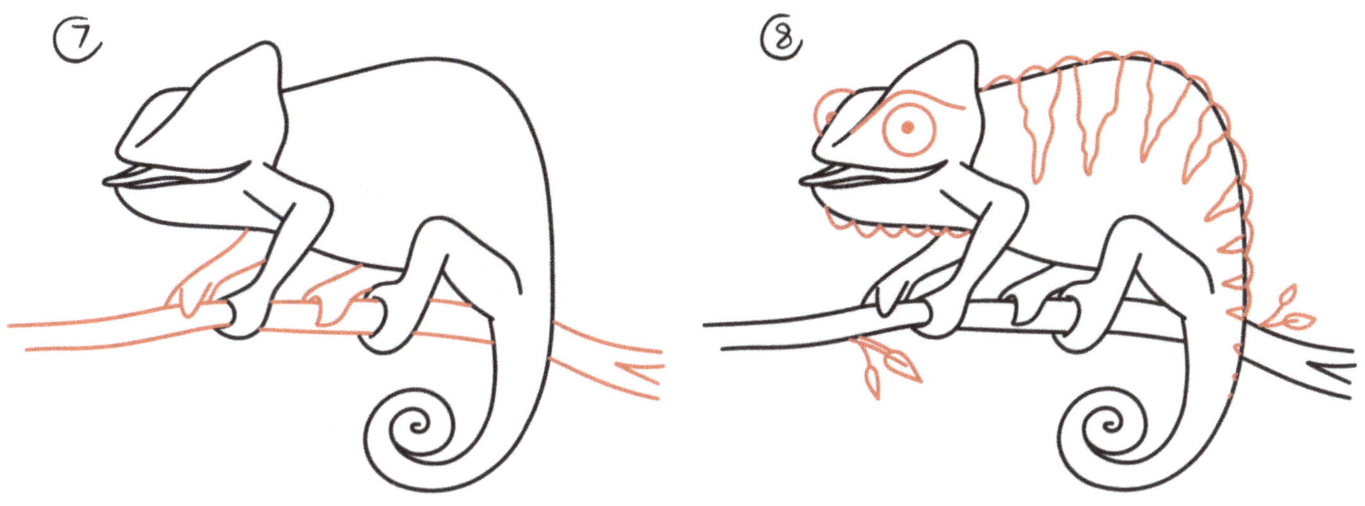

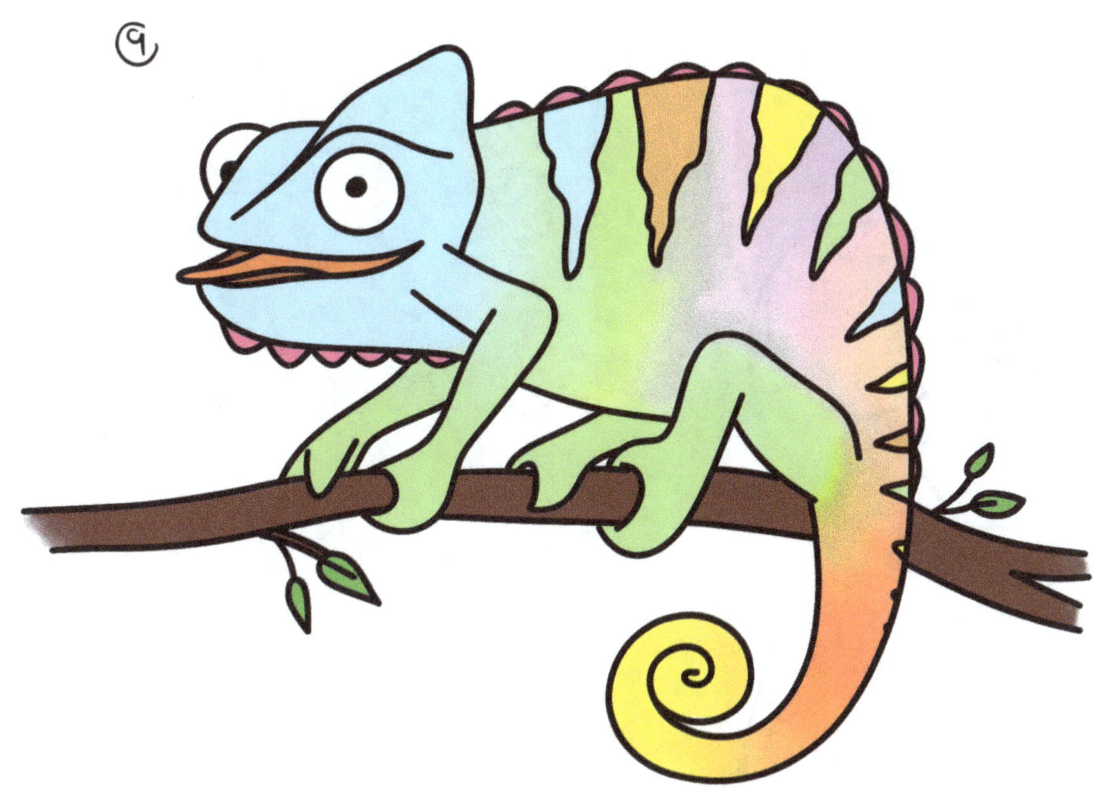

SEAHORSE

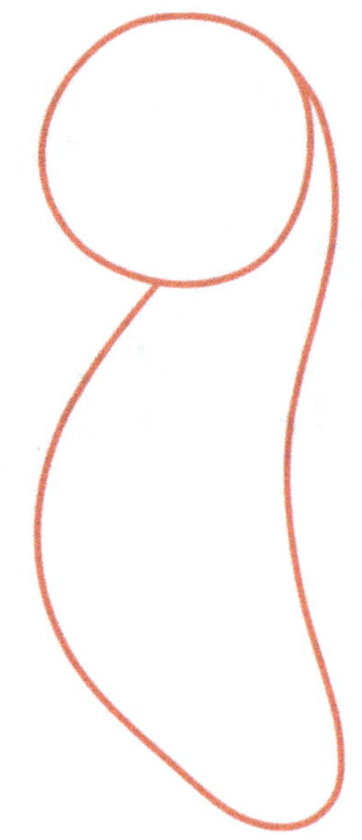

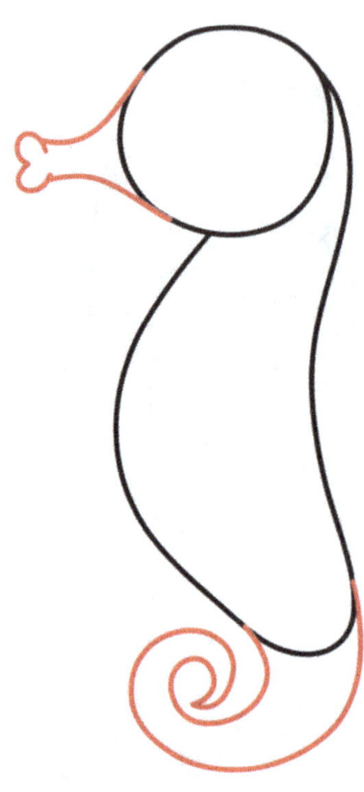

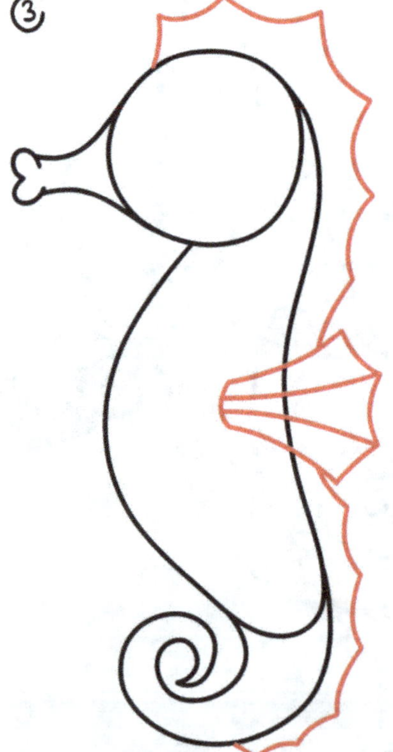

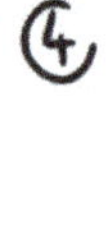

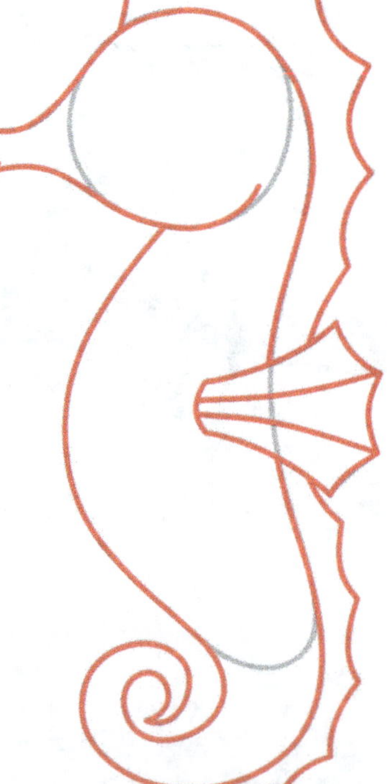

SEAHORSE

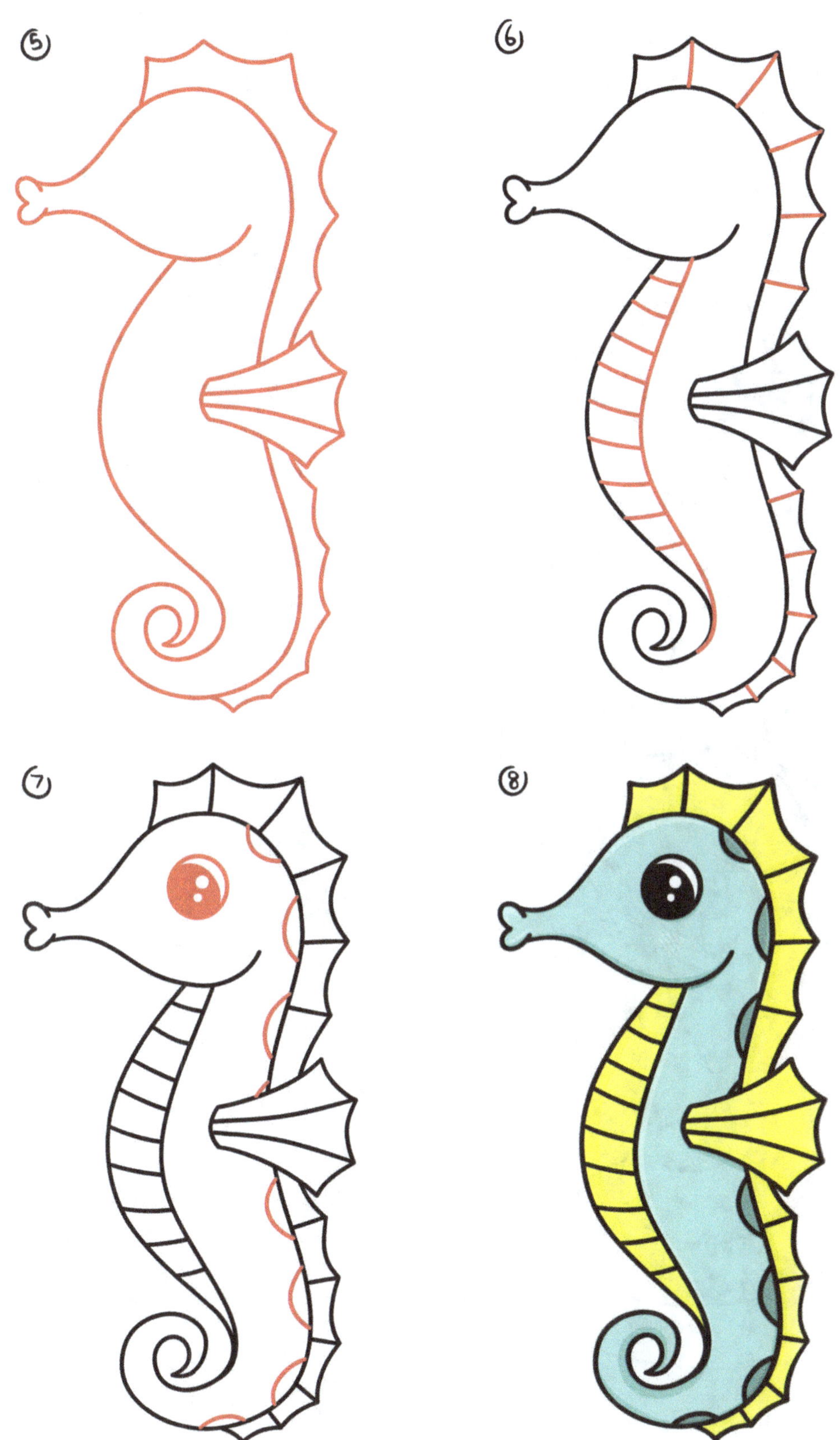

SNAKE

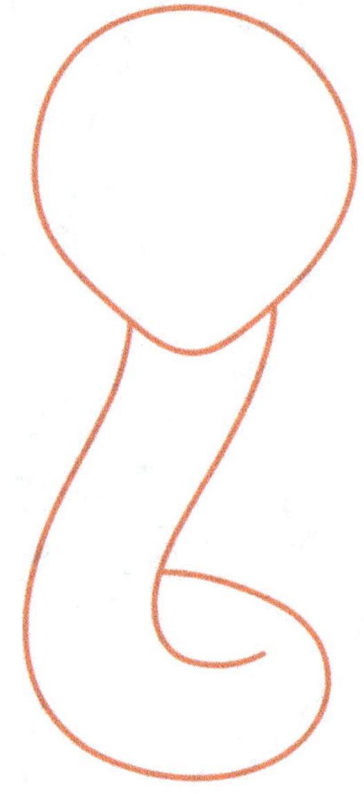

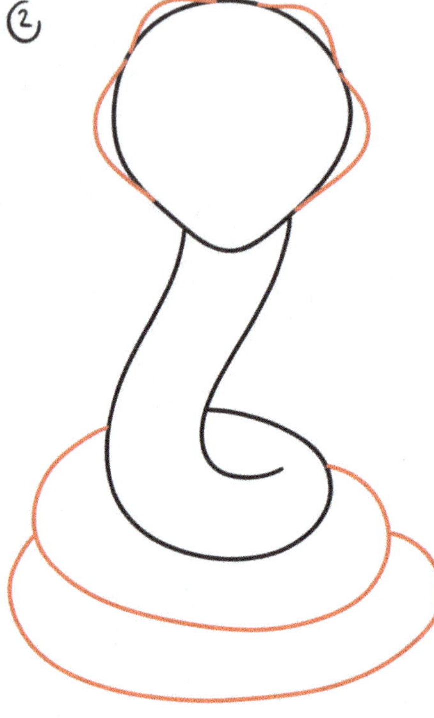

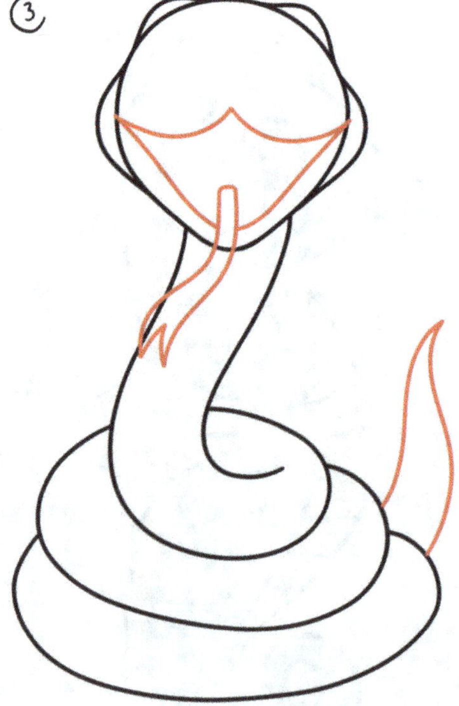

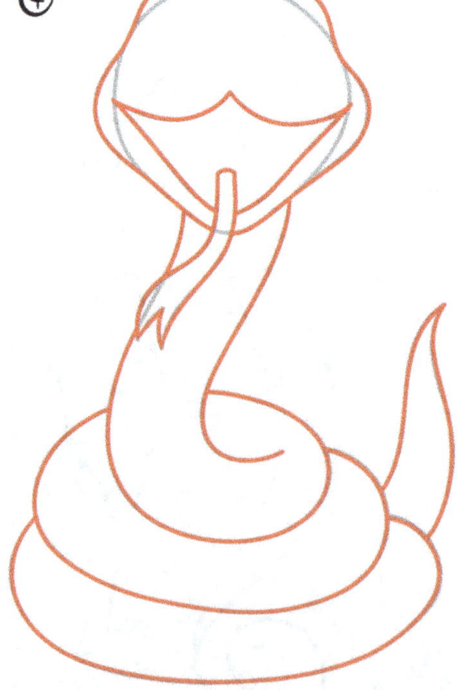

SNAKE

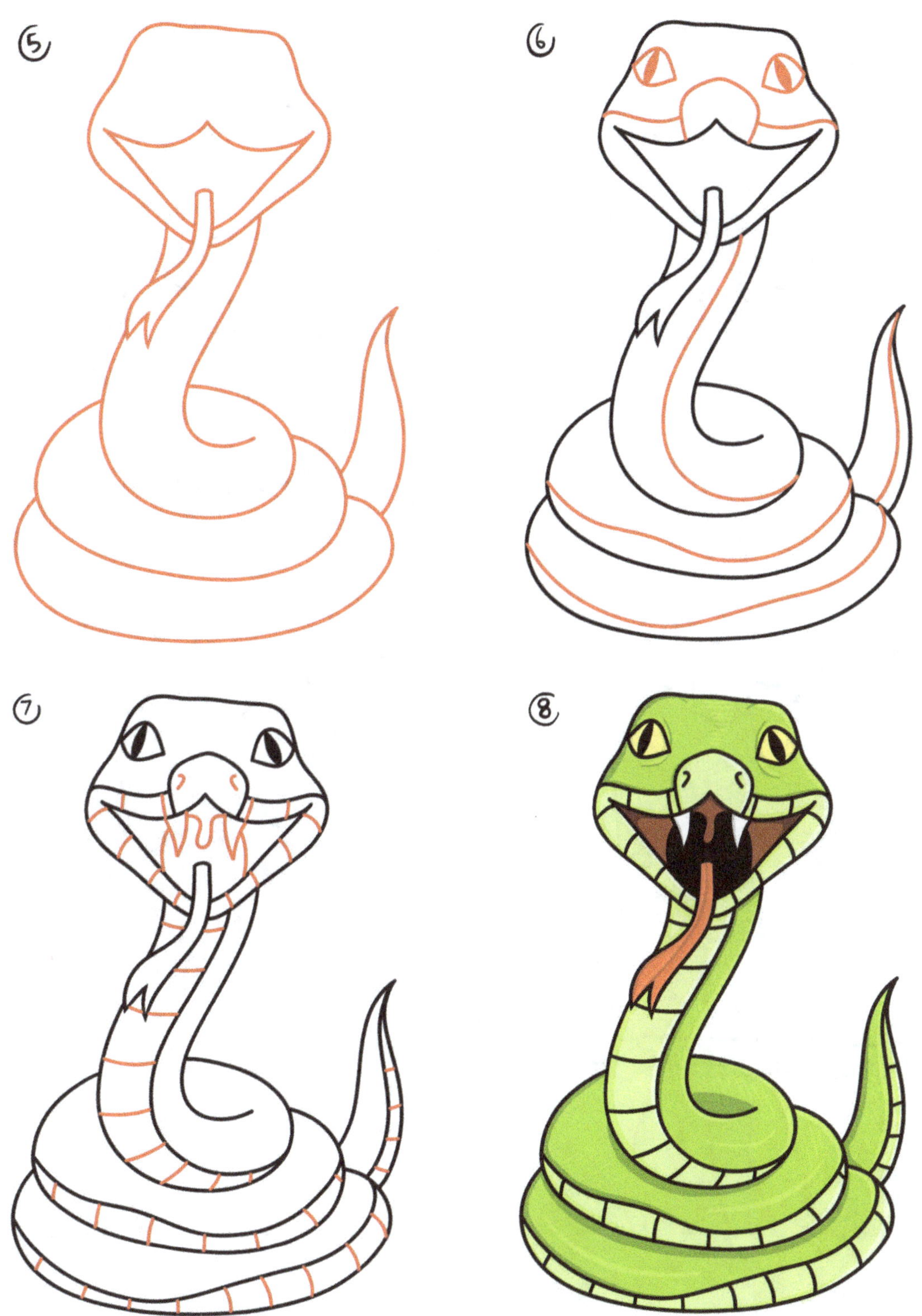

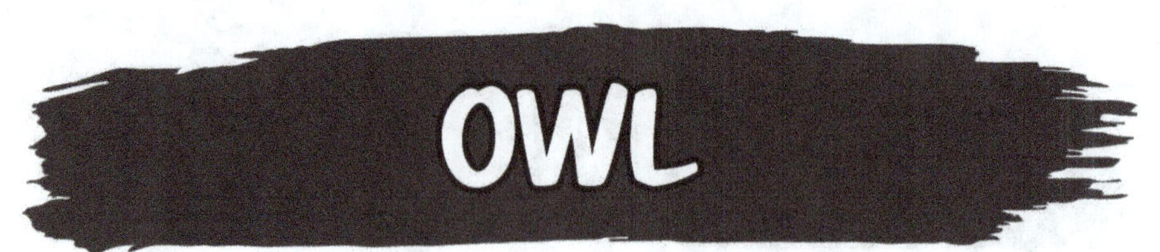

① ②

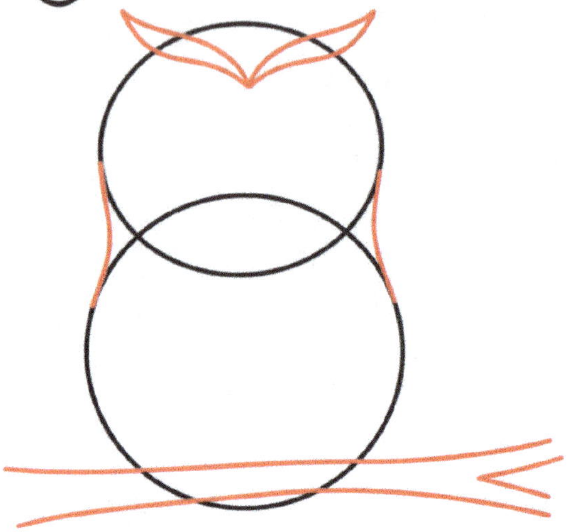

③ 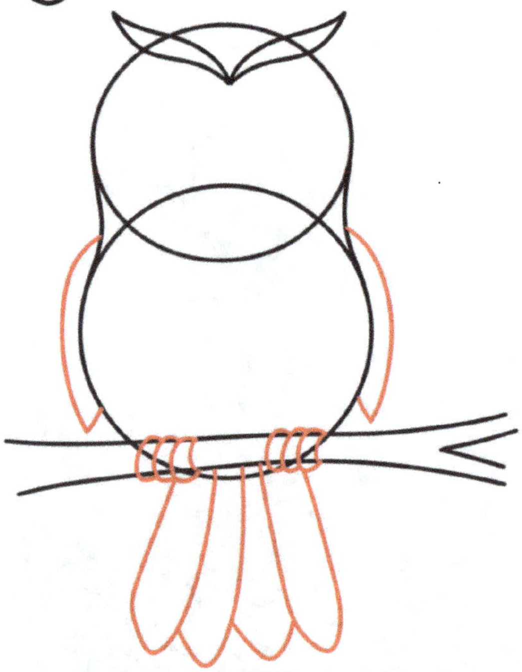 ④

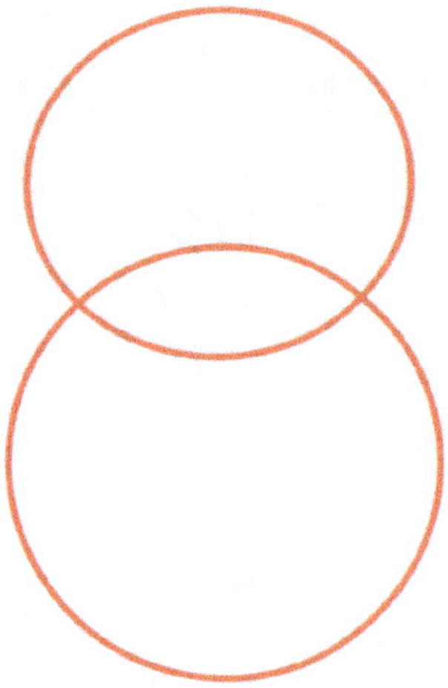

58

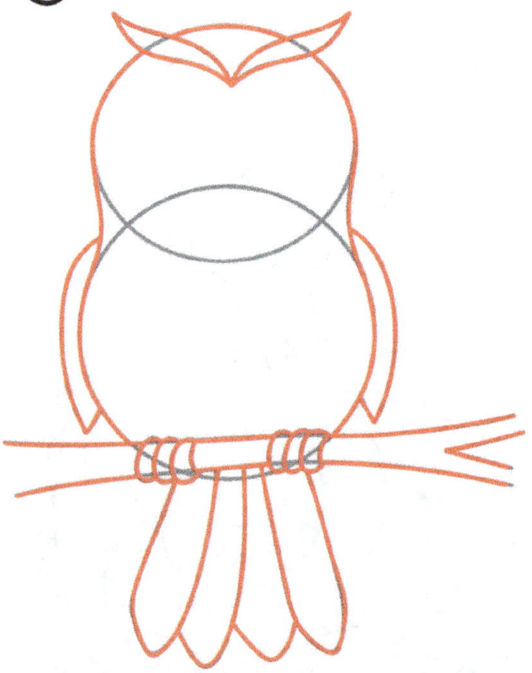

OWL

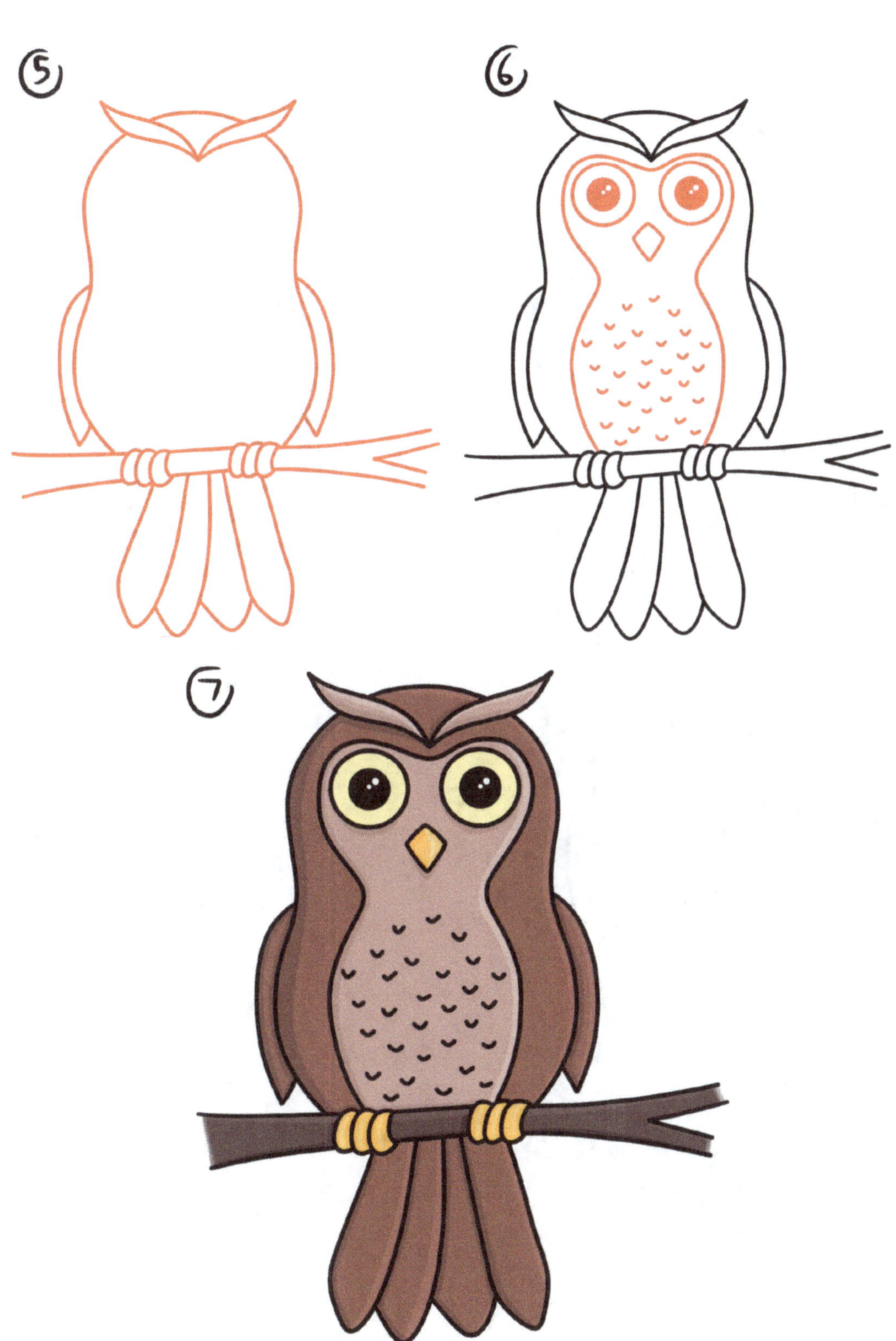

DOG

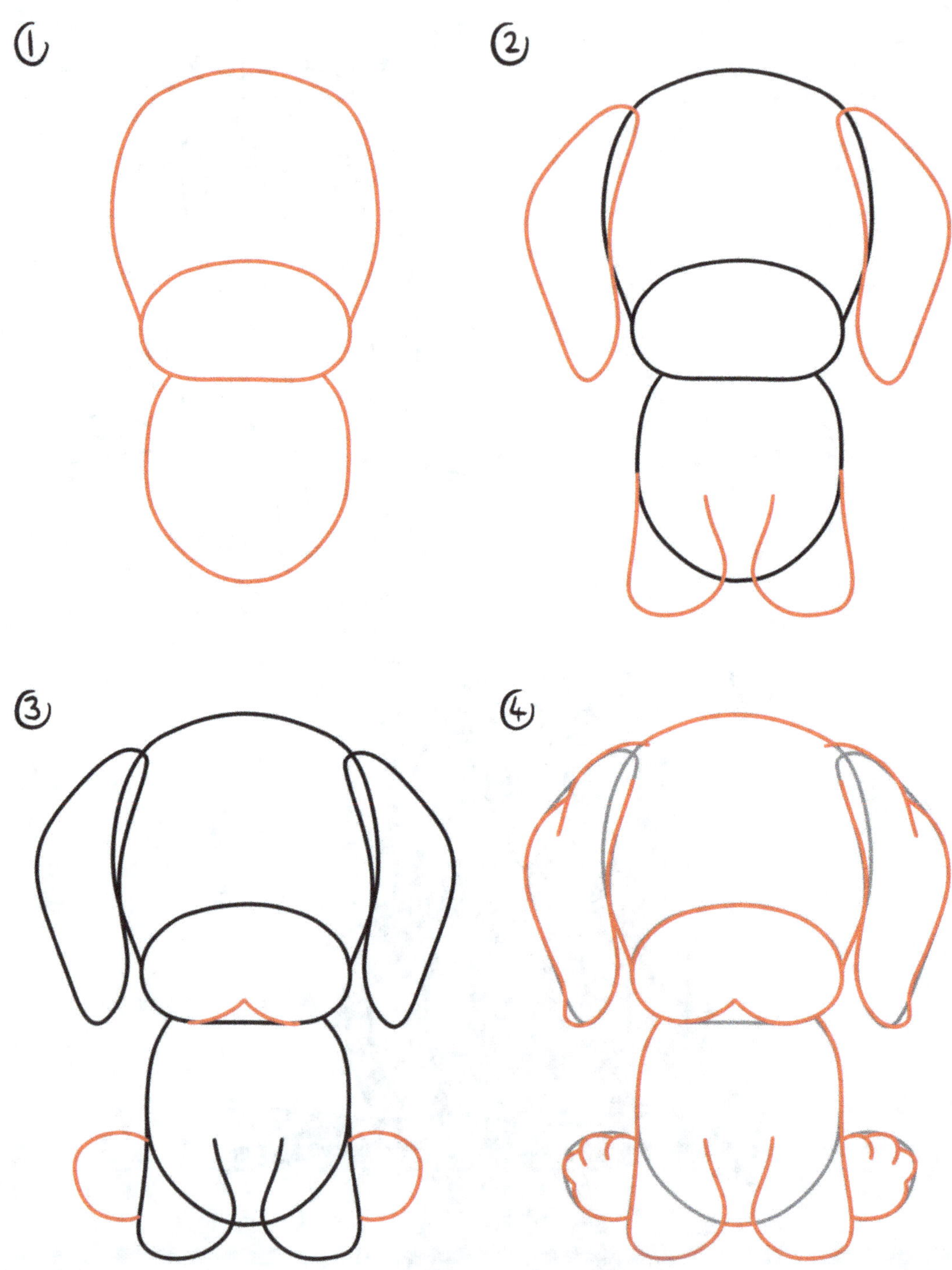

DOG

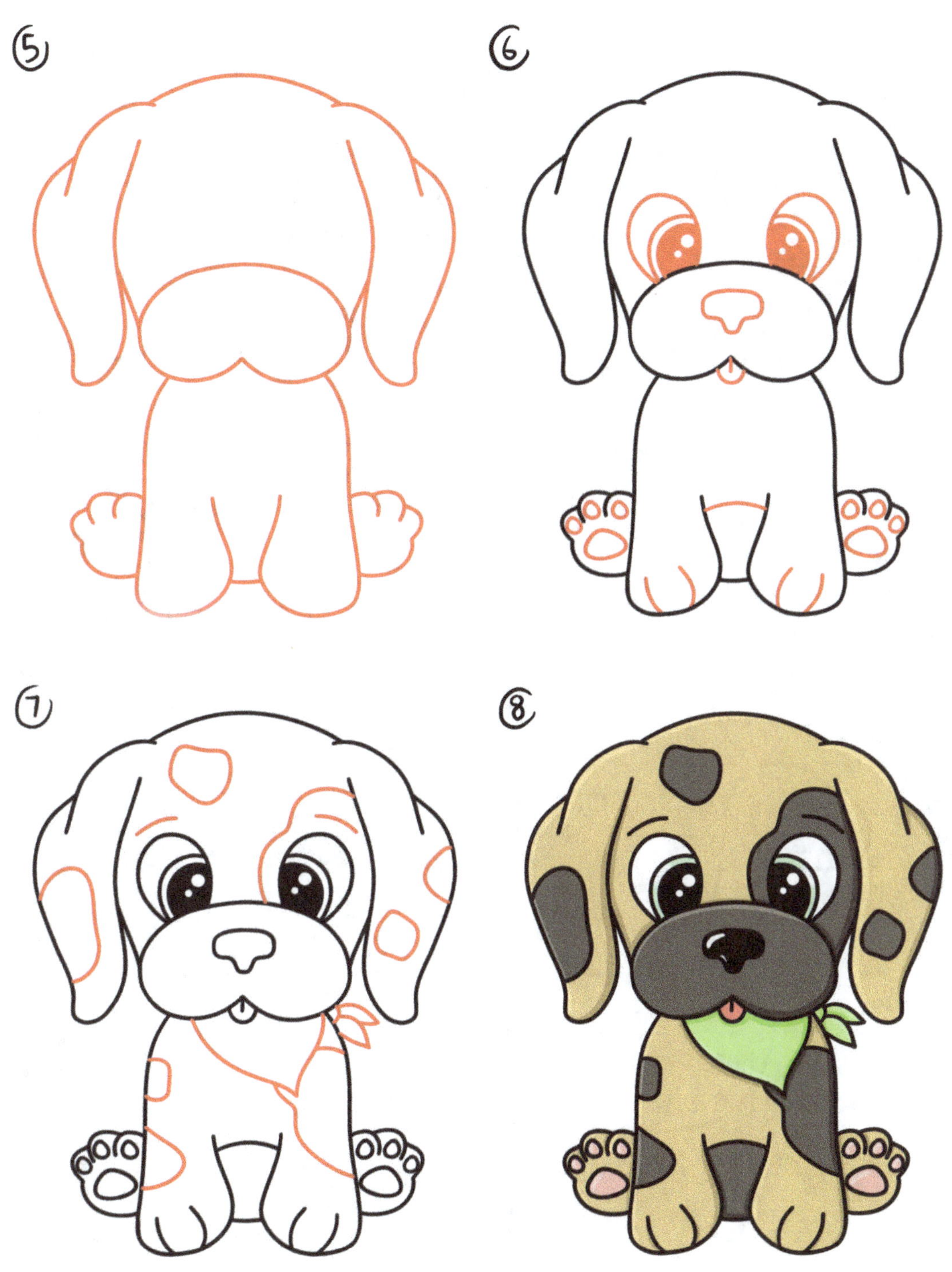

GIRAFFE

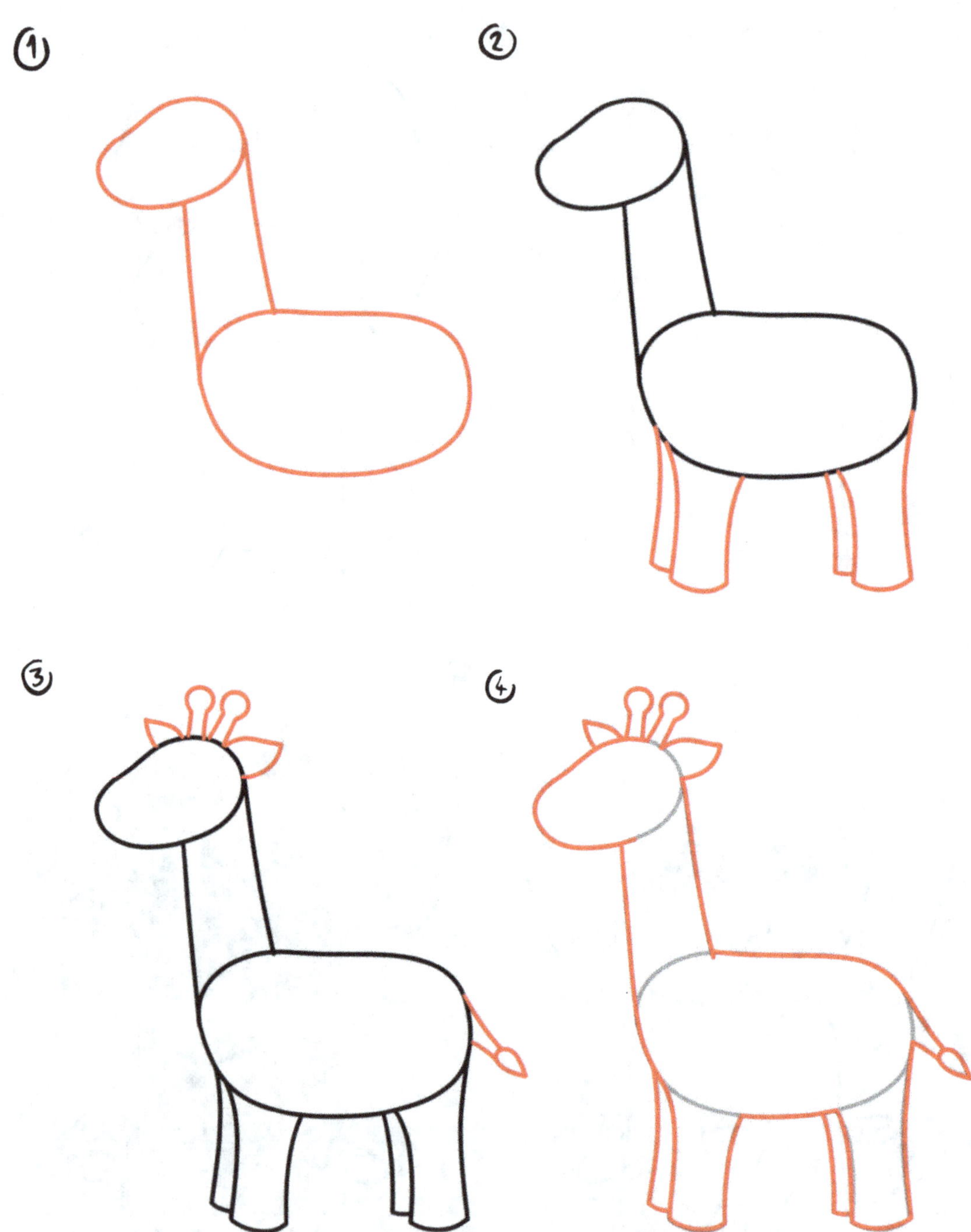

GIRAFFE

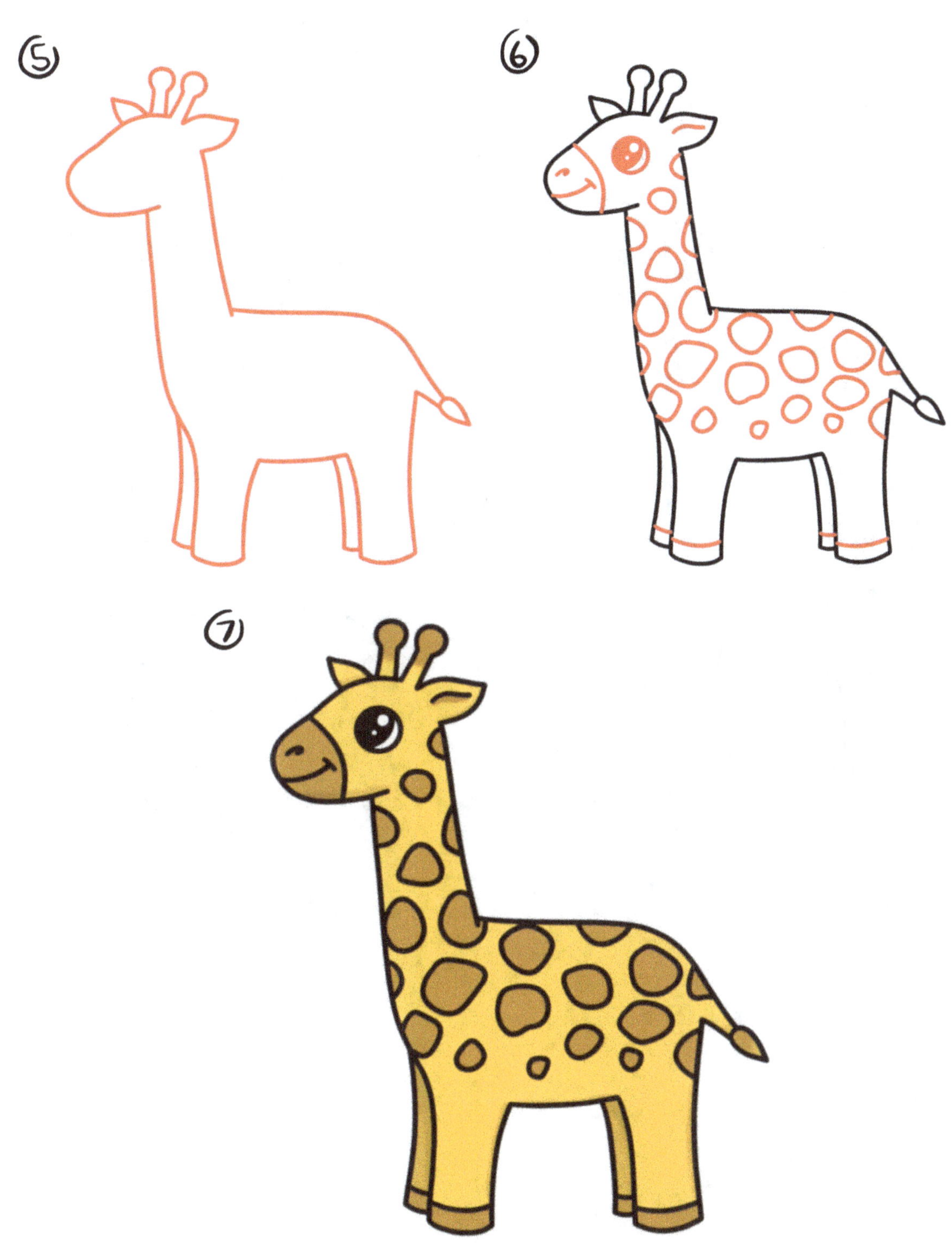

UNICORN

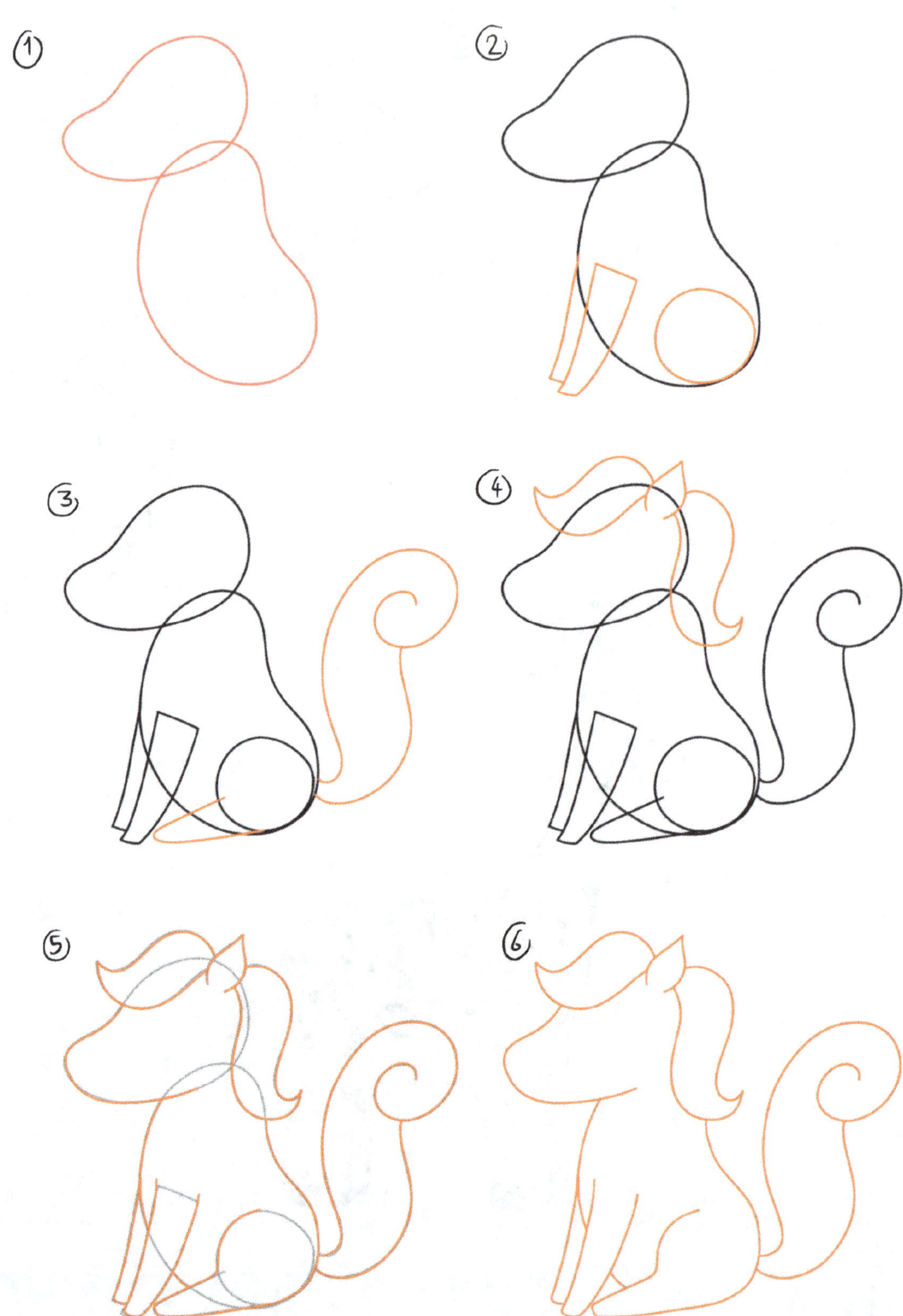

UNICORN

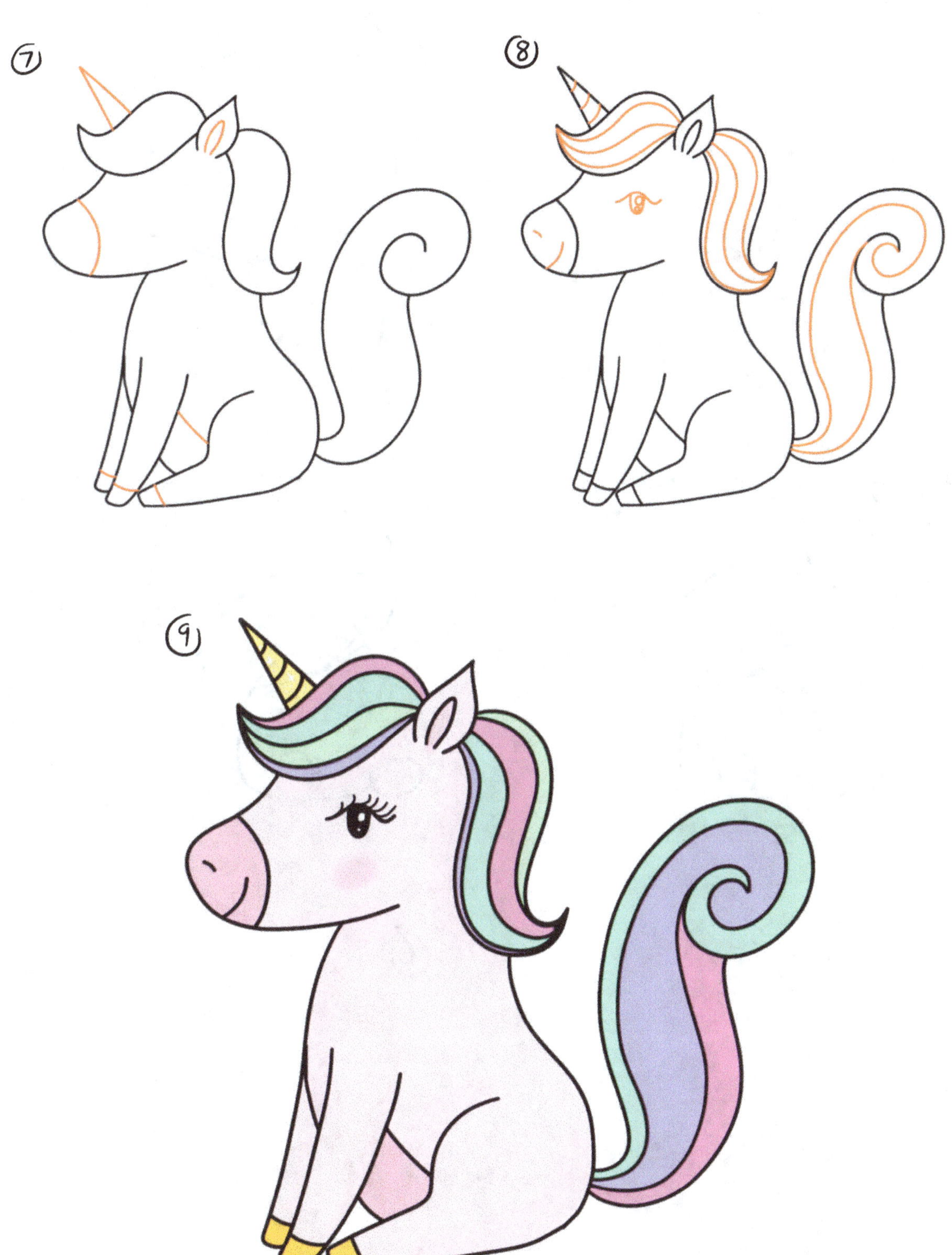

MONKEY

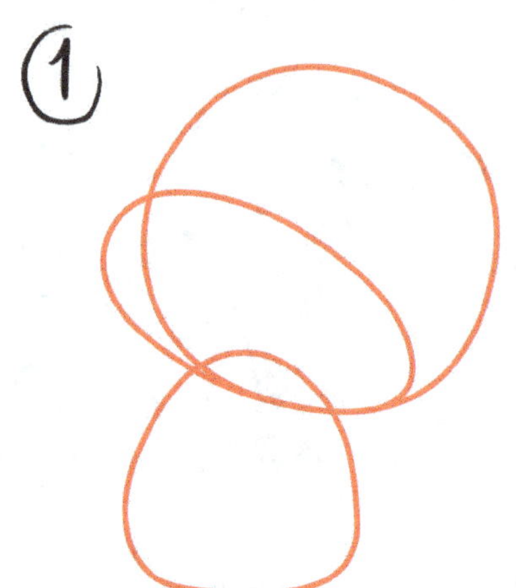

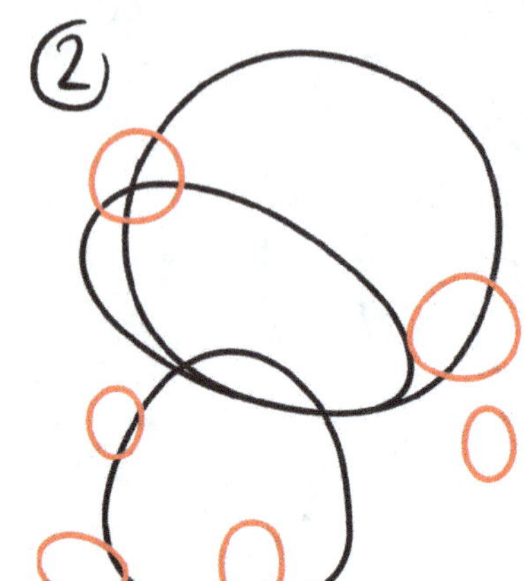

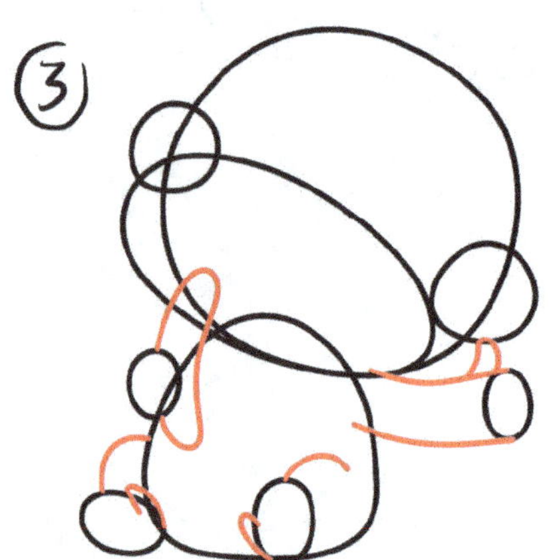

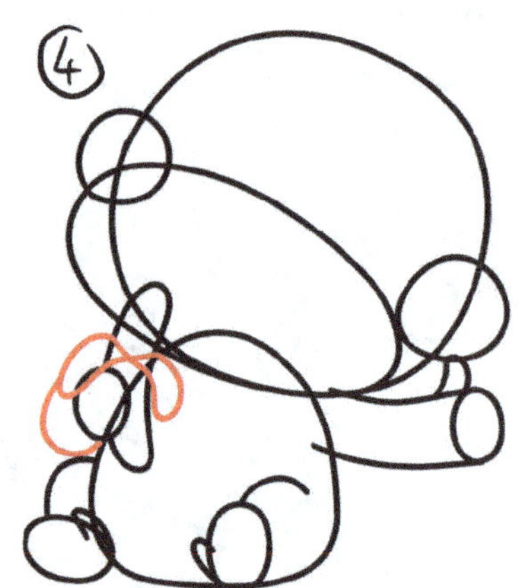

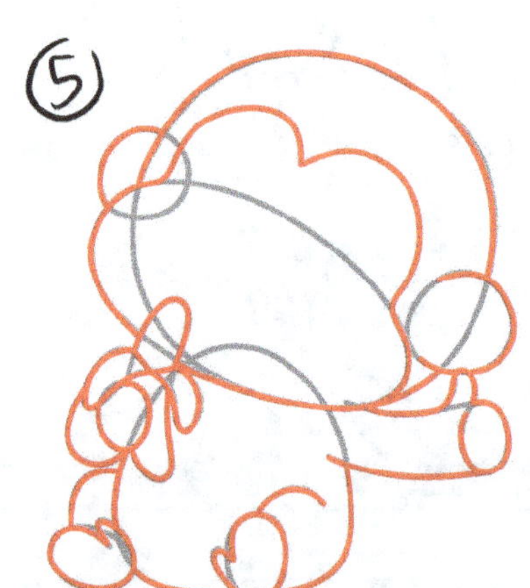

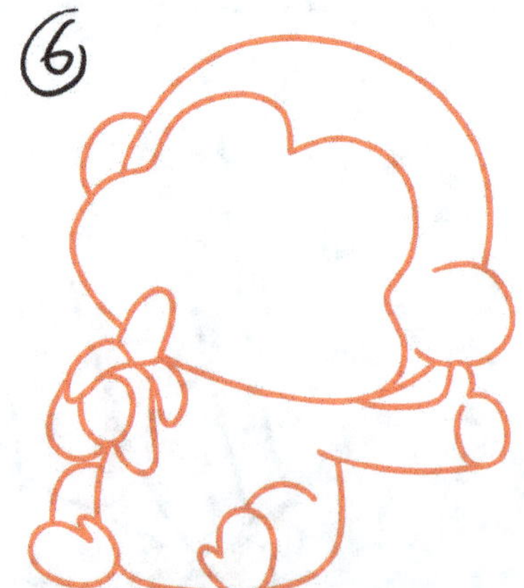

MONKEY

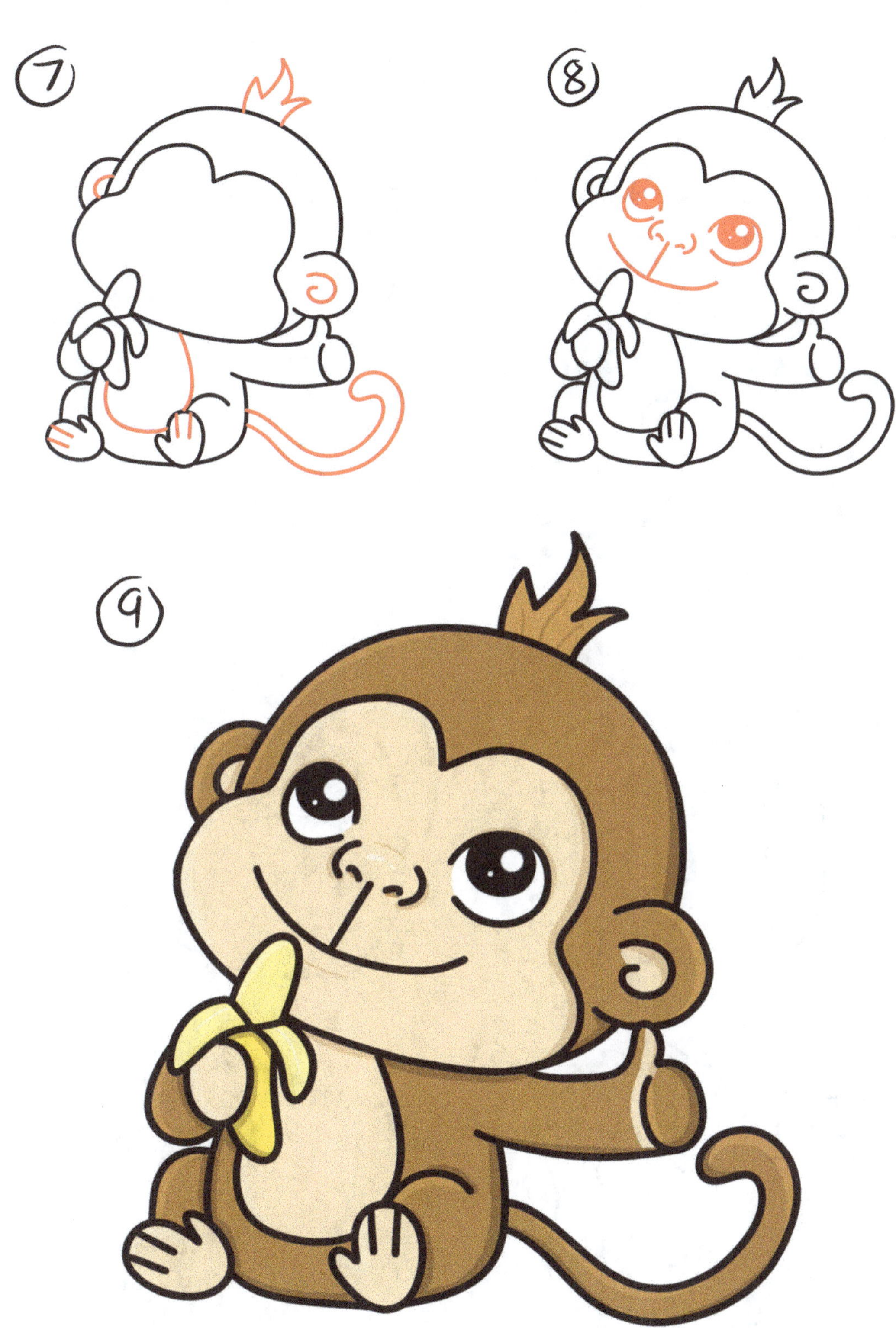

SLOTH

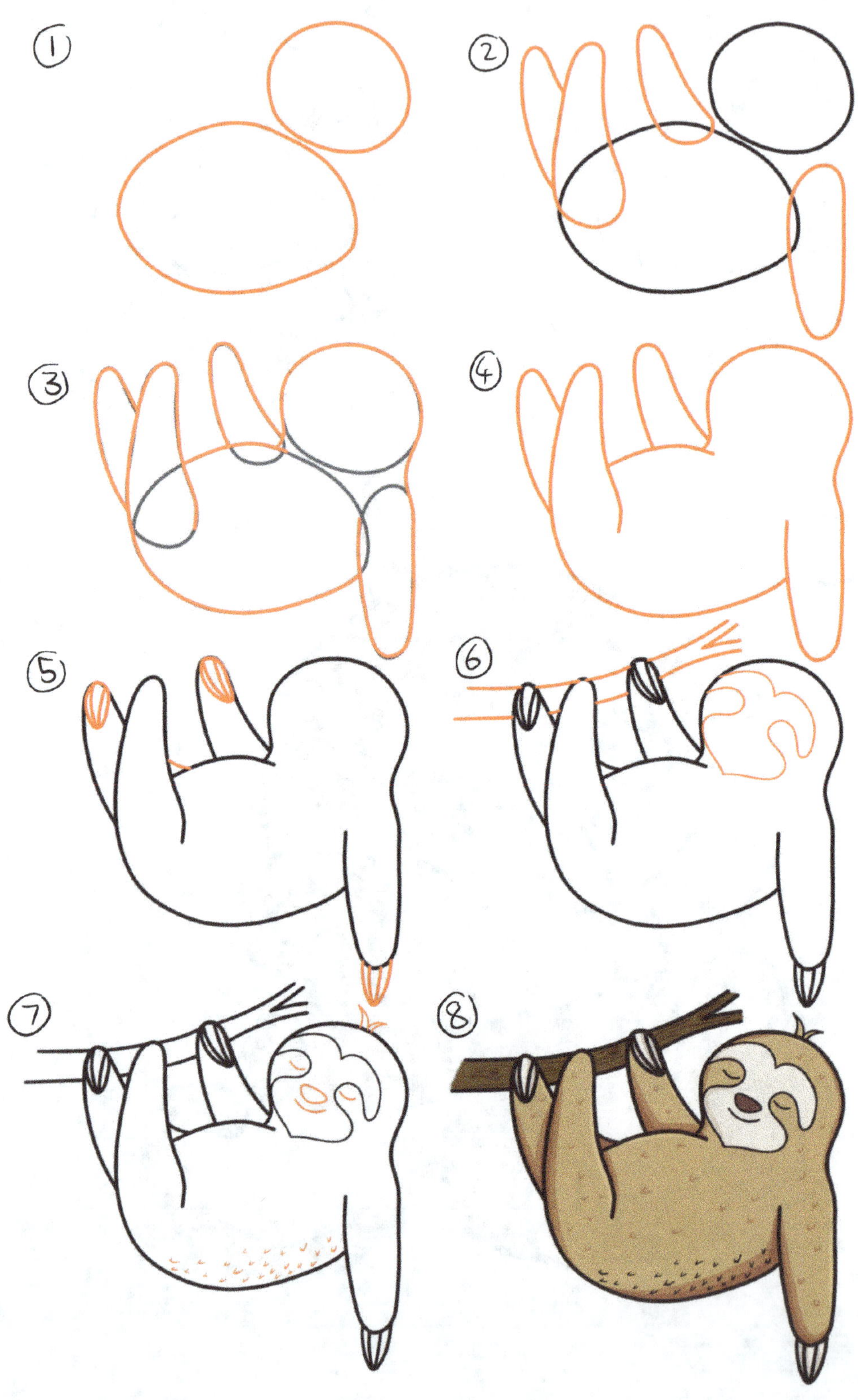

SEA TURTLE

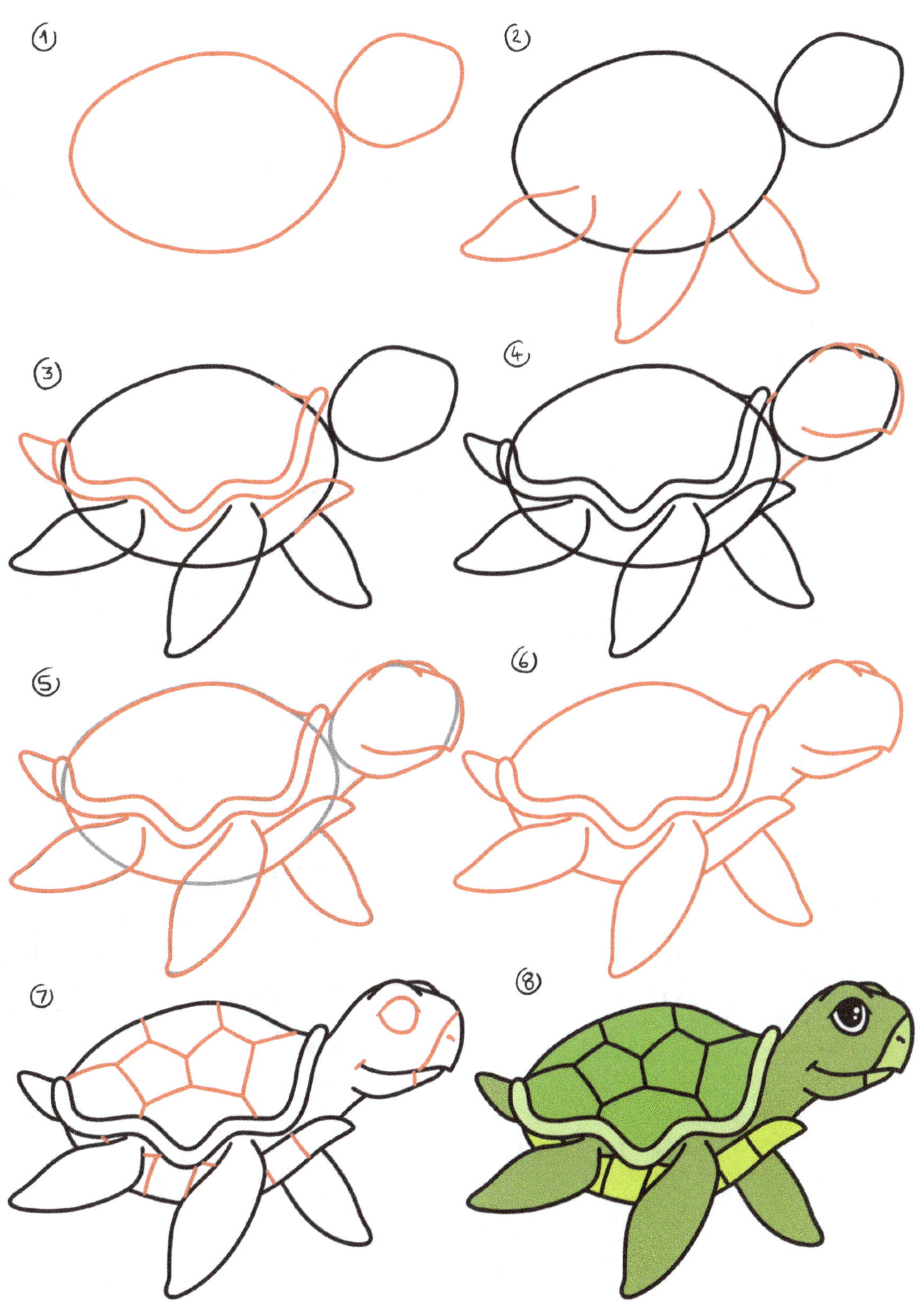

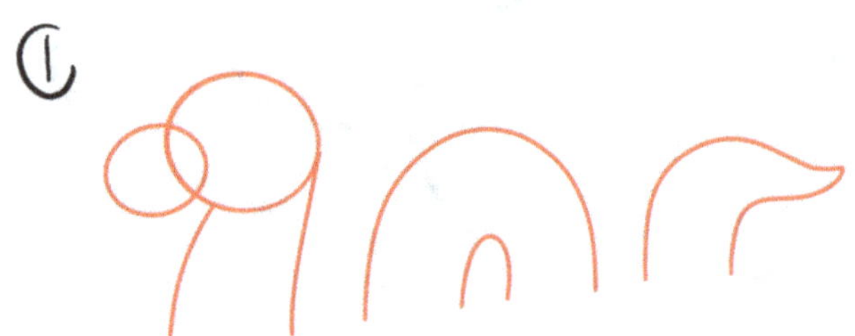

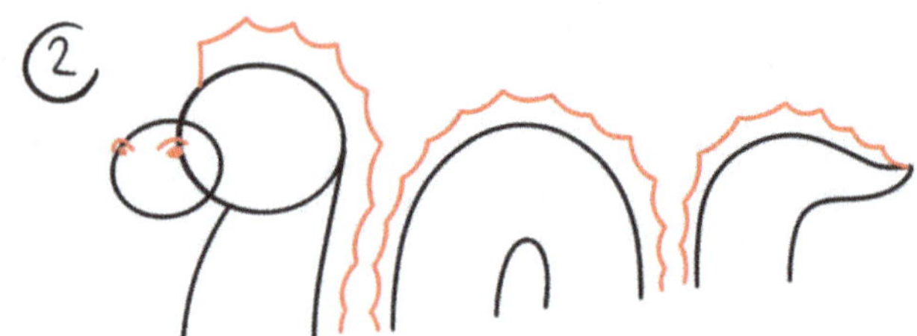

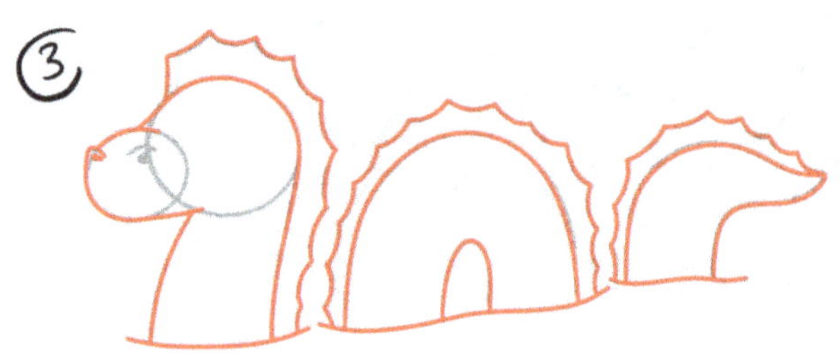

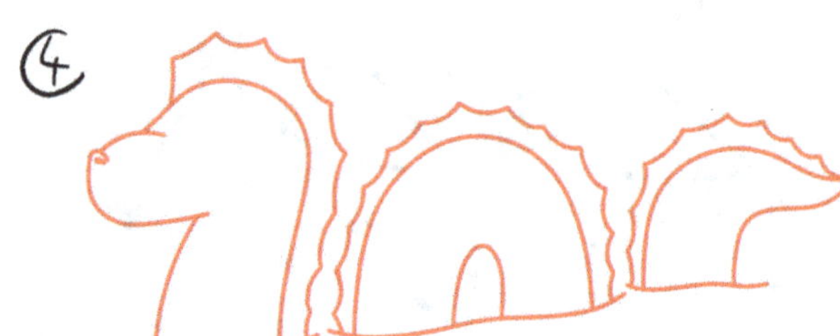

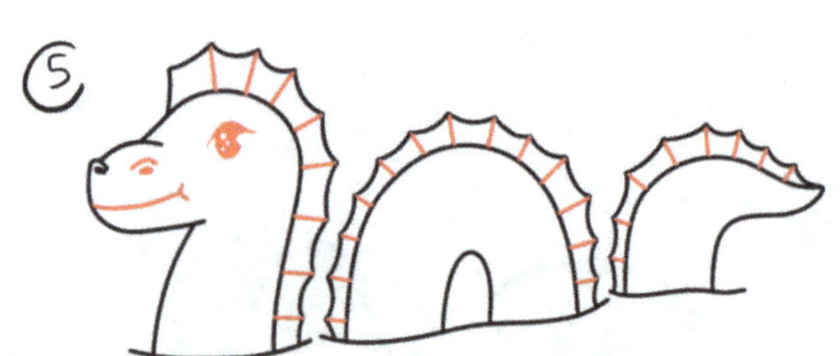

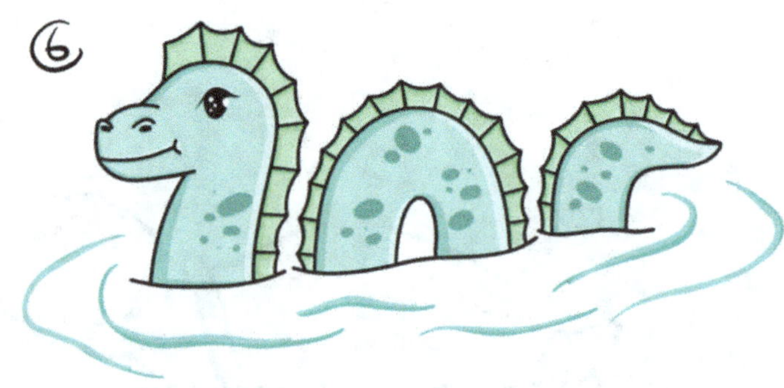

IGUANA

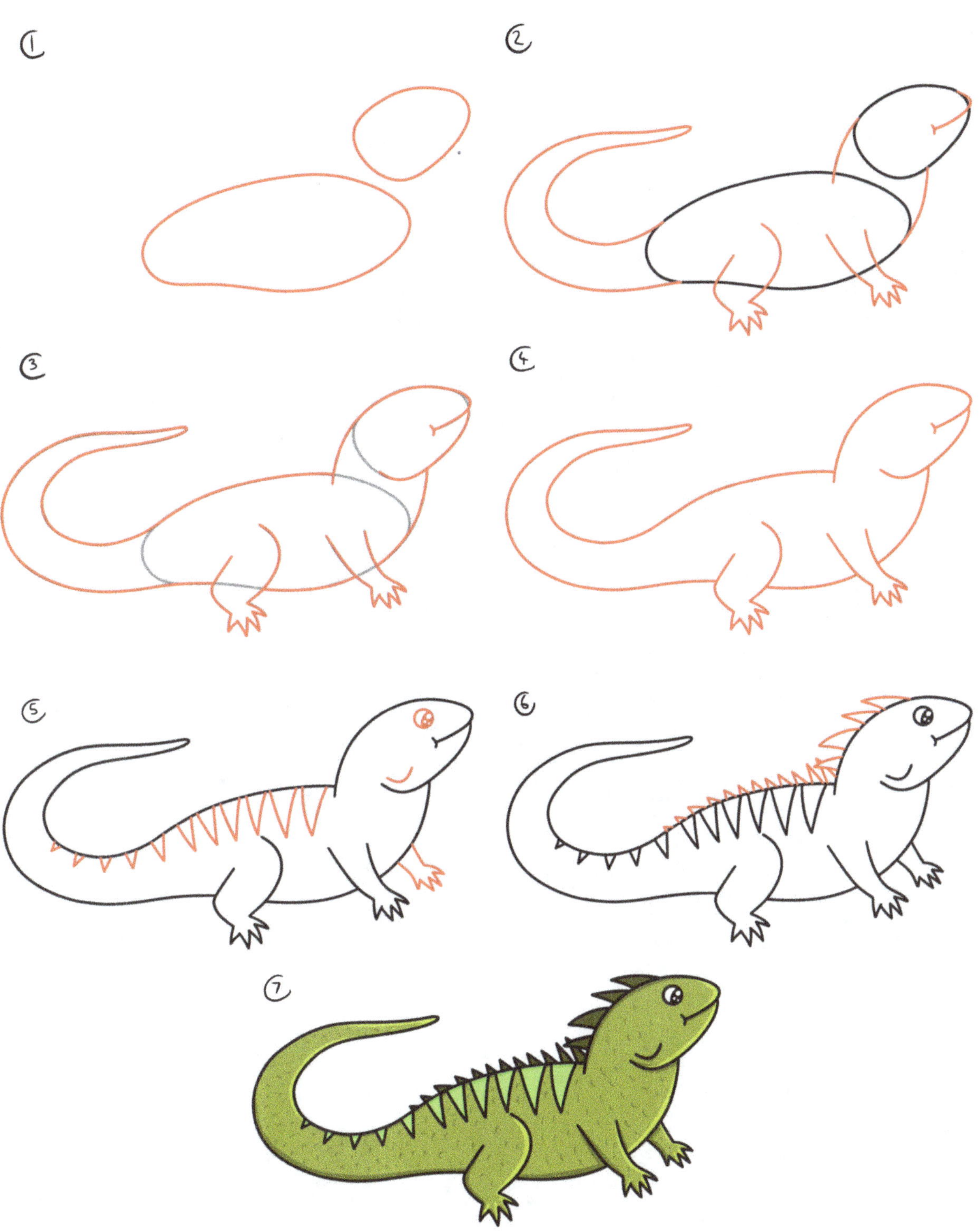